IMAGES
of America

GREENSBORO'S CONFEDERATE SOLDIERS

LINES

Sacred to the Memory of

Capt. Henry C. Gorrell of Greensboro', N. C.,

Of the Second North Carolina Regiment,

Who fell in an attack which he led against the Federal Batteries at the battle of Fair Oaks, June 14, 1862.

MAY HE REST IN PEACE.

They laid him away in the cold damp ground,
On the banks of a Southern stream;
Not far from his home in his own native land
Where the rays of a tropic sun gleam.
No coffin to enclose his mangled remains
No shroud save his uniform coat,
But his name is entwined with the laurels of fame,
And on memory's tablet 'tis wrote.

He sleeps all unheeding the cannon's deep roar,
Or the sound of the murmuring stream;
The armies march o'er him in battle array,
Yet he fears not their musketry's gleam.
For his "home" he fought, for his "rights" he died,
He's a martyr to a "Glorious Cause;"
The Confederacy he loved, and to see her prevail
He died while defending her laws.

In a little white cottage in the land of the South,
They are waiting his coming again:
But dream not that his body all mangled and torn,
Has been laid 'neath the field of the slain.
Sleep, soldier, sleep! in thy rough Southern tomb,
While above thee may soft breezes wave,
And in summer the birds shall thy requiem sing
From the trees over thy "Patriot grave."

BY A FRIEND OF THE CAUSE.

A poem, written as a memorial to Capt. Henry Clay Gorrell, became a folk ballad. Poetry and songs, written in an attempt to express the deep emotional impact of war, tell the stories of many fallen heroes and the pain their families endured at home. Gorrell died instantly, a Yankee's bullet piercing his forehead. His father, Ralph, with the aid of Henry's comrades, retrieved his corpse from the battlefield. (Library of Congress.)

ON THE COVER: Shown on the cover is a reunion picture of Guilford Chapter 795, United Confederate Veterans, photographed in the early 1900s. The building in the background is the First Presbyterian Church in Greensboro, North Carolina. The celebration included a trip to Green Hill Cemetery to honor Confederate war dead and a lavish meal prepared by the women of Greensboro. (Greensboro Historical Museum Archives, Inc.)

IMAGES
of America

GREENSBORO'S CONFEDERATE SOLDIERS

Carol Moore

ARCADIA
PUBLISHING

ISBN 978-0-7385-5401-3

Published by Arcadia Publishing
Charleston SC, Chicago IL, Portsmouth NH, San Francisco CA

Printed in the United States of America

Library of Congress Catalog Card Number: 2007943612

For all general information contact Arcadia Publishing at:
Telephone 843-853-2070
Fax 843-853-0044
E-mail sales@arcadiapublishing.com
For customer service and orders:
Toll-Free 1-888-313-2665

Visit us on the Internet at www.arcadiapublishing.com

This book is dedicated to my family in Kentucky and the wonderful people in North Carolina that treat me like family.

CONTENTS

ACKNOWLEDGMENTS

Foremost, I wish to thank individuals who donated pictures but wish to remain anonymous.

Individuals who submitted pictures are gratefully acknowledged: Jack Brame, Col. John Sloan Camp 1290, Sons of Confederate Veterans; Jane Lopp Brame, Guilford Chapter 301, United Daughters of the Confederacy and Order of Confederate Rose; Benjamin Briggs, Preservation Greensboro, Inc.; Chalmer Clapp Jr.; William "Bill" Jones, Col. John Sloan Camp 1290, Sons of Confederate Veterans; Michele Norman Miller, Guilford Chapter 301, United Daughters of the Confederacy; Keith Osborn; Don Saunders, commander, Col. John Sloan Camp 1290, Sons of Confederate Veterans; Joanne Sharpe, president, Guilford Chapter 301, United Daughters of the Confederacy; and Mike Whitfield.

A warm thank you is extended to Etta Farrar Taylor Mangum. For going beyond the call of duty and copying images for use in this book, Jack and Jane Lopp Brame humbled me with their generosity. William "Bill" Jones offered cherished pictures as well as valuable information from his many years of research. Maggie Bullwinkel and Arcadia Publishing are greatly appreciated for the work they do preserving history for future generations. For the love and support bestowed upon me by Julianne and David Moore, Rick and Darlene Ramey, Carol Whitfield, Randall Clapp, Peppy, Flake, Milkshake, and Poor Mc, I am grateful.

ABBREVIATIONS USED IN THIS BOOK:

James W. Albright, ALBRIGHT
Jack Brame, BRAME
Jane Lopp Brame, LOPP
Benjamin Briggs, Preservation Greensboro, Inc., PG
Betty Caldwell, CALD
Chalmer Clapp Jr., JR
Walter Clark, CLARK
Greensboro Historical Museum Archives, Inc., GHMAI
Greensboro Public Library, GPL
Keith Osborn Collection, KEITH
Library of Congress, LOC
North Carolina Office of Archives and History, NCA
University of North Carolina at Chapel Hill, UNC
Greensboro Lodge No. 76, Earley W. Bridges, EB
Documenting the American South, University of North Carolina at Chapel Hill Libraries, North Carolina Collection (docsouth.unc.edu), DOC
Greensboro Daily News, GDN
University of North Carolina, Charlotte, UNCH
William "Bill" Jones, JONES
Mary A. Long, LONG
Michele Norman Miller, MNM
Carol Moore, CAM
National Archives, NA
Don Saunders, DS
John Wells Simpson, JW
John A. Sloan, SLOAN
Sallie Stockard, NCMA
The First Hundred Years of Historic Guilford by A. Earl Weatherly, EW
Joanne Sharpe, JS
Mike Whitfield Collection, WHIT

INTRODUCTION

In the days preceding the War Between the States, Greensboro was a quiet town. People were patriotically proud to be citizens of the United States. The residents of Greensboro, located in the heartland of Guilford County, North Carolina, were especially proud of their ancestry and the roles their forebears performed in the founding of the United States. They were, and are, especially proud of their community's involvement in a major battle during the Revolutionary War that occurred in Guilford County on March 15, 1781.

Greensboro, named in honor of Gen. Nathanael Greene, became the county seat of Guilford in 1808. To understand the mind-set of Greensboro's residents on the eve of the War Between the States, one needs to understand the history of the community. The citizens are an independent and freedom-loving people. Before the War Between the States, the citizens honored the war veterans of the Revolutionary War, celebrated George Washington's birthday, paraded on the Fourth of July, and celebrated the anniversary of the Battle of Guilford Courthouse annually.

The Greensboro *Patriot*, a local newspaper, focused on issues concerning the nation and brought issues to the attention of the citizens of Greensboro in the years preceding the War Between the States. Sen. John Adams Gilmer of Greensboro, an active representative in Washington, D.C., informed the town's residents of alarming situations developing in the nation. Situations in the United States in 1860 were such that Greensboro's citizens felt the need to reestablish the local militia. The former militia, the Greensborough Guards, was formed in 1840 for the protection of the community, and the members spent most of their time practicing drills and performing in parades to the delight of the townspeople.

In 1860, the citizens once again felt the need for protection, and the Guilford Grays were organized to protect the community. The Guilford Grays consisted of men of all ages, Caucasian and African American, free and enslaved, married and single, from all occupations—physical laborers to schoolteachers, to the leading people of the community. They all united for the common cause of protecting the community.

The militia was established on January 9, 1860, with 37 charter members. On March 15, 1860, the officers received their commissions from Gov. John W. Ellis and adopted this date, the anniversary of the Battle of Guilford Courthouse, as their date of organization. The militia's first weapons were smoothbore muskets supposedly used during the Revolutionary War. Their uniforms, manufactured in Philadelphia, included a single-breasted frock coat with two rows of buttons, pants with a black stripe, a black leather belt, and a cap. The students of Greensboro Female College presented the officers of the Guilford Grays with swords.

On May 5, 1860, the Guilford Grays participated in their first public parade. The parade began in front of the courthouse and proceeded west on Market Street to Edgeworth Female Seminary. James Turner Morehead's daughter, Mary "Miss Mamie" Morehead, the newly crowned 1860 May Day queen, presented the Guilford Grays with a beautiful banner designed by the Weir family of Greensboro. The banner was manufactured in Philadelphia. Greensboro, like most Southern communities, relied on the northern United States and foreign countries for most of their manufactured goods.

In the summer of 1860, the Guilford Grays enjoyed parades and participated in memorial activities, including a monument dedication at Alamance Church Cemetery in honor of Col. Arthur Forbis, who died while leading North Carolina troops at the Battle of Guilford Courthouse. At the time of the Guilford Grays' organization, many communities throughout the South were organizing militias in fearful anticipation of possible conflicts.

The year 1861 brought changing days to Greensboro. Concerns abounded that the United States planned to send federal troops to Southern forts. Despite these conflicts, the Guilford Grays continued to entertain the citizens of Greensboro. In February 1861, the Guilford Grays paid honor to Pres. George Washington by celebrating his birthday. The first anniversary of the organization of the Guilford Grays, March 15, 1861, was a day of celebration in high style.

In 1861, Greensboro was a stronghold of determined Unionists. Pres. Abraham Lincoln's election spread alarm. Gen. Pierre Gustave Toutant Beauregard's attack on Fort Sumter in South Carolina meant war, but it was President Lincoln's call for troops that overwhelmed the hearts of all North Carolinians. North Carolina governor John W. Ellis pointedly responded to U.S. secretary of war Simon Cameron, "You can get no troops from North Carolina."

On April 17, 1861, Governor Ellis ordered the Guilford Grays to Fort Macon. The future Confederate soldiers were full of life and laughter, but many of the townspeople expressed deep concern at the thought of what might occur to their young men. The women of Greensboro went to work forming committees to support the young men.

The first Confederate soldiers from Greensboro to die in the service of state and country met defeat by disease, not bullets. Greensboro's Confederate soldiers entered the service of the Confederate States of America with excitement, honor, and dedication to their homes and families. For most of the soldiers, the reason they entered and fought was for the home hearth. They considered themselves foremost North Carolinians and secondly United States citizens.

The issues of slavery, though acknowledged, were not the driving force behind Greensboro's military. The fact that Abraham Lincoln won the presidential election of 1860 was not the reason Greensboro's citizens chose to fight for the Southern cause. The people of Greensboro were heartbroken on the day their beloved state chose to sever its relationship with the United States. No one can claim more patriotism for the unity of the country on the eve of the Civil War than the state of North Carolina and the citizens of Greensboro. The goal of the Greensboro's soldiers was simply to protect their families and homeland.

Vigilante groups organized in Greensboro. These men went door-to-door to determine the residents' position on the events occurring locally and nationally. Fear, in some cases, played a role in townspeople's responses.

The Guilford Dixie Boys, Company M, 21st North Carolina, organized on June 4, 1861. The Guilford Light Infantry, Company C, 45th North Carolina, and Company B, 45th North Carolina, known as Capt. Charles E. Shober's Company, enlisted in Greensboro in 1862. The Guilford Minute Men, Company E, 22nd North Carolina, consisted mainly of men from Greensboro and Guilford County. Capt. A. P. McDaniel advertised in the Greensboro *Patriot* newspaper for men to do their duty and enlist before being drafted. His company became Company A, 53rd North Carolina. Capt. David Scott Jr. raised a company of men for Company D, 53rd North Carolina. Company F, 54th North Carolina was named the "Stonewall Boys" in honor of Gen. Thomas "Stonewall" Jackson. The "North State Boys," Company K, 45th North Carolina, consisting of men from Guilford County and neighboring Forsyth, Davidson, and Rockingham Counties, enlisted in 1862.

Cavalry regiments from the Greensboro area were known as the Guilford Cavalry, Capt. John E. Wharton's Partisan Rangers, and Capt. Nathaniel P. Rankin's Partisan Rangers.

Home guards were established for the protection of the community. Col. James R. Cole commanded the 4th North Carolina Regiment Home Guard. With most adult males absent from the community, young boys served as the town's defense. One company was under the command of Capt. John W. Pitt. As the war progressed, a senior guard was established. Capt. Jacob Boon's Company and Capt. W. B. Johnston's Company provided service as senior reserves. Later in the war, the invalid corps was formed for home defense. The invalid corps consisted of maimed or sick men who could no longer endure the tribulations of active warfare. Early in the war, injured and sick men were relieved from duty entirely, but due to shortages of able-bodied men as the war progressed, those with physical infirmities were needed to serve in any capacity they could.

Some of Greensboro's young men enlisted in Virginia regiments. As the war progressed and the availability of new recruits shrank, a few North Carolina regiments merged with regiments from other states.

Some men were exempt from military duty because their jobs were more important than their service as soldiers. Railroad employees, inventors, pharmacists, gun manufacturers, pastors, and local government officials were often exempt from duty. A few men paid substitutes to enlist in their place.

Greensboro's Confederate soldiers, during four years of fighting, found themselves at war with the United States, disease, hunger, and poverty, all equally deadly. Death became a constant reality in the lives of the soldiers and residents. Though death may not have sent its lethal calling card directly to a soldier, he witnessed his comrades in arms dying brutally on the battlefields and feverishly from horrible diseases. For many of the soldiers, their military life consisted of spending days—which turned into years—in Northern prisons, where many suffered from abuse from Yankee soldiers and the treacherous northern winters. Some soldiers' service to the fledgling Confederate States of America ended quickly. They lay, forgotten and unknown, buried on the battlefield. The veterans that survived to return to Greensboro found filth, poverty, and anger.

The horrid scenes the soldiers witnessed changed them forever. Visions of swollen dead bodies, streams flowing bloodred and brothers and friends dying haunted them, and the smells of battle—the stench of burning flesh, burning trees, and decaying animals—nearly suffocated them. The physical demands put upon the soldiers—extreme hunger, forced marches, tainted water, and frigid winters endured sometimes without shoes—pressed the physical limits of the men; some suffered from the physical effects of war their entire lives. Psychological nightmares from the sights and sounds of minié balls, grapeshot, and canisters splintering trees and human bodies alike amid the chaos of battle haunted many of the men, but the most horrifying sounds were the screams of wounded men of both armies crying in pain, begging for help and water, before finally surrendering to death. Often the last thoughts of these young men were of home and family, their sole reason for sacrificing their life upon the battlefield.

Trains carrying troops and supplies passed through Greensboro daily. The returning trains brought injured soldiers and news from the battlefield. Townspeople met each train to read casualty lists. Women brought what food they could gather to share with the injured troops as they passed through Greensboro. Mourning garments became the style for most women in Greensboro as the war progressed.

By 1862, the people of Greensboro were regularly hearing of the death of a local young man. Supplies continued to be sent in support of the war; even a church bell was donated to the cause. The years 1863 and 1864 brought more death, more hunger, and more suffering to soldier and citizen alike. In October 1863, the beloved Guilford Grays were nearly obliterated at the Battle of Bristow Station. The siege of Petersburg, Virginia, in 1864 brought more dead Confederate soldiers to Greensboro for heartbroken family members to bury. Worried minds thought of peace and longed for an end to the cruel war. Families found their hearts torn between hoarding their food in hidden walls, attics, and barns or sending it to their starving sons and husbands in the service of their fledgling country.

In the spring of 1865, Greensboro was a riot of activity. The people were hungry; it was incomprehensible to them that Confederate and state commissaries, located in Greensboro and at train depots in several communities near Greensboro, were packed with food and supplies that were rotting while their children were starving and in need of clothing and blankets. The women of Greensboro attempted to take matters in their own hands. Greensboro's Confederate soldiers met them with weapons loaded and aimed directly at them in an attempt to stop the rioting and pillaging occurring throughout town.

Gen. Joseph E. Johnston's Army of Tennessee, consisting of over 90,000 men surrendered in North Carolina. Johnston chose Greensboro to bid his troops farewell. Remnants of Johnston's army camped in and around Greensboro. They, too, deserve the title of Greensboro's Confederate soldiers.

After the surrender, Federal troops occupied Greensboro. The war-worn Confederate soldiers that survived the horrific war returned to Greensboro broken in all regards. Many lost arms and legs in the lost cause of the Confederate States of America. They came home to poverty, to suffer a decade of governmental control under the guise of the Reconstruction Act. For many, the insult was too much to bear; there was no work or money. Many of Greensboro's veterans traveled west to start their lives anew. Many of the soldiers died after the war from the effects of disease and, in some cases, from the effects of vaccinations received during the war. The townspeople suffered as well; a Yankee officer slapped down one Greensboro woman.

Very little is written of the African Americans, free or enslaved, in the annals of Greensboro history. James W. Albright wrote in his book, *Greensboro 1808–1904*, that those in bondage held steadfast in their dedication to their masters during the war years. Many of the slaves performed duties for their masters throughout the war. A few of those enslaved served with and were Confederate soldiers from Greensboro.

Capt. John A. Sloan, in his book *Reminiscences of the Guilford Grays*, paid honor to "Bill," a family servant that, in Sloan's opinion, served throughout the war honorably and deserved mention for his loyalty. John Gilmer, who described himself as "colored," earned a Confederate pension for his service in the Confederate army. Many emancipated slaves continued to reside in Greensboro with their former masters and worked for them their entire lives.

The women of Greensboro, who fought on the home front for survival, realized their capacity to survive, thus adding confusion for the returned veterans. The women did not stop after the war but continued their work through benevolent societies and memorial activities, culminating in 1899 with the formation of Local Chapter 301, United Daughters of the Confederacy.

The War Between the States is known by many names—the War for Southern Independence, the Civil War, and the Great Rebellion, to name a few—but by whatever name the Late Unpleasantness is called, it evokes the passions of people throughout time.

One

The Guilford Grays

Capt. John Alexander Sloan (1839–1885) served in the Guilford Grays from its organization in 1860 until the company surrendered in 1865. He wrote *Reminiscences of the Guilford Grays: Co. B, 27th NC Regiment* and *North Carolina in the War Between the States*, recording for posterity the history of the Guilford Grays and North Carolina. The Grays' banner has "Greys" inscribed upon it. (GHMAI.)

Shown is a bookmark found on the inside cover of *The Book of Parlour Games*, written in 1858, from the library of James W. Albright. The book contains directions for acceptable games men could play with women. The young men of Greensboro in 1860 looked forward with exuberant dreams for the future—dreams of home and family that, unbeknownst to them, would soon be shattered. (CAM.)

On March 15, 1860, the 79th anniversary of the Battle of Guilford Courthouse, Governor Ellis tendered commissions to the officers of the Guilford Grays militia. Militias in Guilford County existed before the Revolutionary War. Shown is a remnant of the flag presented by the students of Edgeworth Female Seminary in 1840 to the Greensborough Guards, the predecessor of the Guilford Grays. (NCMA.)

The Guilford Grays met each Friday night on the second floor of an old cotton mill to perfect their marching skills in anxious anticipation of the parades and memorial services in which they planned to participate. Their guidebook was *Scott's Tactics*. May Day celebrations at Edgeworth Female Seminary excited them greatly; it was rumored they were to be presented a banner. Shown is Tate's Mill. (WHIT.)

On a sun-drenched day, May Day queen Mary Morehead presented a banner, saying: "In the name of my subjects, the fair donors of Edgeworth, I present this banner to the Guilford Grays. Feign would we have it a 'banner of peace,' and have inscribed upon its graceful folds 'peace on earth and good-will to man.'" The Mary Morehead Chapter of the Order of Confederate Rose honors Mary. Shown is her monument. (CAM.)

The flag, 6 feet by 5 feet in size and made of blue silk, has a painting of North Carolina's coat of arms circled by a wreath of oak leaves and acorns with an eagle above it and the motto "E Pluribus Unum" inscribed on a scroll and below that the words "Greensboro, North Carolina." The original flag is stored at the Museum of the Confederacy in Richmond, Virginia. (GHMAI.)

Henry Gorrell (shown) received the banner on behalf of the Guilford Grays. He pledged, "We, the Guilford Grays, do here beneath its graceful folds pledge our lives, our fortunes, and our sacred honor, and swear for them to live, them to love, and, if need be, for them to die." Gorrell honored his pledge in 1862, shot dead in the forehead by an enemy's bullet. (GDN.)

On July 4, 1860, the Guilford Grays rode wagons to Alamance Church to honor Col. Arthur Forbis of North Carolina, who died at the Battle of Guilford Courthouse in 1781. The Reverend Eli W. Caruthers opened the service. Later Caruthers (shown) lost popularity with the men of Greensboro when he openly denounced the war. He felt the men were engaging in a cause that was wrong. (CALD.)

The Guilford Grays continued to perform patriotic duties, celebrating George Washington's birthday in February 1861. Greensboro's citizens, proud of the role their ancestors had played in the formation of the United States, annually celebrated the anniversary of the Battle of Guilford Courthouse. It is with the same patriotism that they chose to defend their homes from Northern aggression. Shown is a statue of General Greene at the Guilford National Battleground Military Park. (CAM.)

James A. Long (shown) gave a speech discussing the events occurring nationally. South Carolina seceded in December 1860, with Mississippi, Florida, Alabama, Georgia, Louisiana, and Texas seceding shortly thereafter. Concern replaced the once happy persona of the troops and the citizens of Greensboro. Long would never know the outcome of the events surrounding his community. He died in 1864 of consumption. (LONG.)

The *Patriot* newspaper recorded, "Our streets are filled with excited crowds, and addresses were made during the day. These speeches all breathed the spirit of resistance to tyrants, and our people were told that the time has come for North Carolina to make common cause with her brethren of the South in driving back the abolition horde." Robert P. Dick, a community leader, (shown) first spoke for the war, but he had a change of heart as the conflict progressed and later advocated peace. (CALD.)

General Beauregard, in command of the Confederate army in Charleston, South Carolina, ordered his troops to open fire on Fort Sumter on April 12, 1861. Pres. Abraham Lincoln immediately requested 75,000 troops to quell the rebellion. Governor Ellis of North Carolina received a telegram from the U.S. secretary of war, Simon Cameron, requesting two regiments. Shown is a Currier and Ives lithograph depicting the interior of Fort Sumter. (LOC.)

Governor Ellis (shown), shocked at the request, stated, "You can get no troops from North Carolina." He immediately ordered the Guilford Grays to report to Fort Macon. The Grays boarded the train in Greensboro on April 18, 1861. Though the townspeople cheered, the look of worry was upon their faces; tears were openly shed. (UNC.)

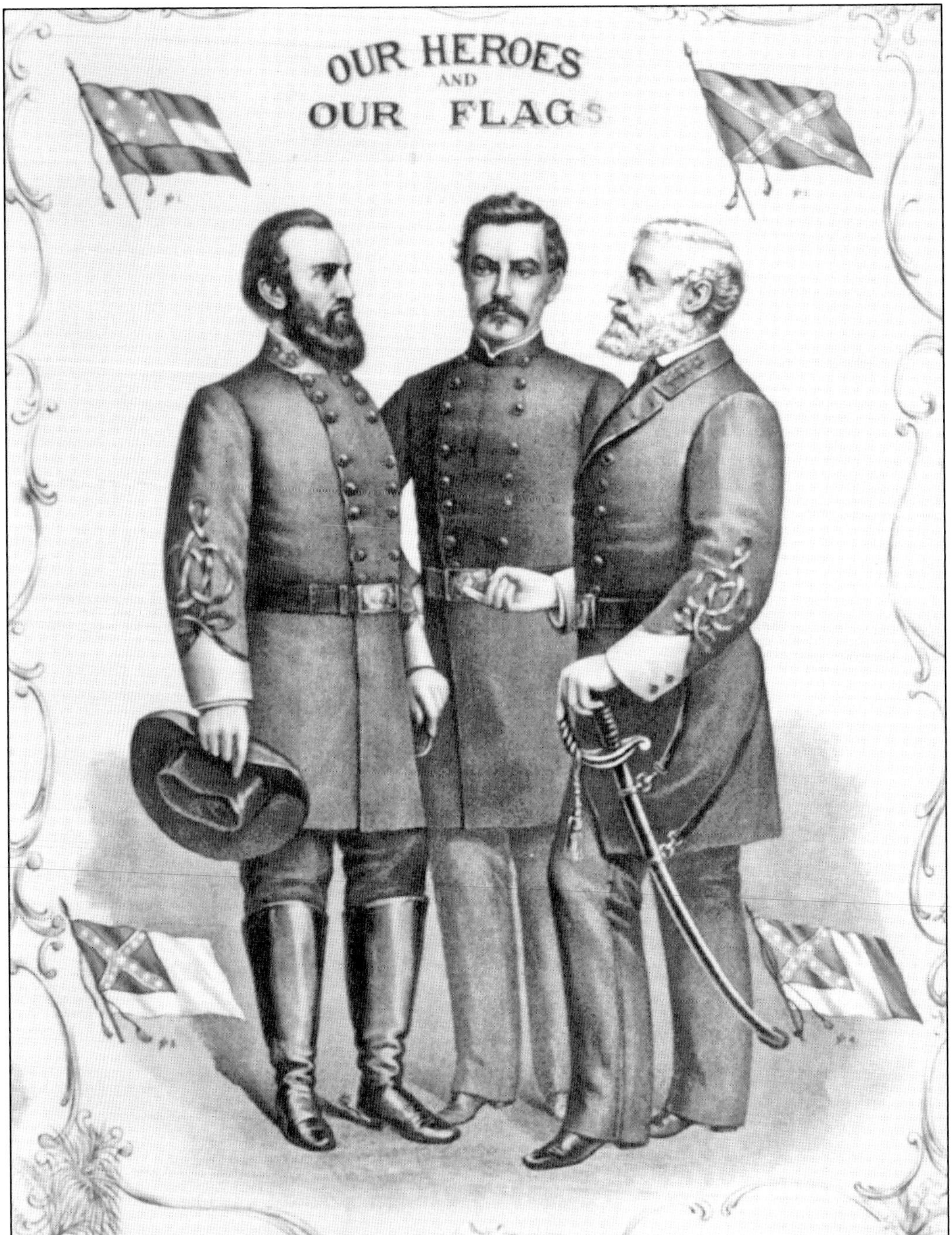

Shown from left to right are Thomas "Stonewall" Jackson, P. G. T. Beauregard, and Robert E. Lee. The flag at upper left is the first Confederate flag, "the Stars and Bars;" the rectangular flag at upper right is the second Confederate naval jack; similar to the Southern Cross flag, it is recognized today as the battle flag of the Confederate States of America. At lower left is the second Confederate flag, "the Stainless Banner," and at lower right is the third Confederate flag. (LOC.)

Two

Company B, 27th North Carolina

The Guilford Grays—Company B, 27th North Carolina—were the first company of men from Greensboro to leave home in defense of their state. John Adams Gilmer (shown) told the Grays to go forth and defend North Carolina whether the enemy came from the north or the south. He openly berated South Carolina for perpetuating disunion and war. Gilmer exchanged letters with Pres. Abraham Lincoln in hopes of avoiding bloodshed. Lincoln offered him a cabinet post; Gilmer declined. Gilmer, a strong Unionist, admitted the deep heartache he felt over the divisions in his country and often cried, but his only son, John, served in defense of his beloved homeland. North Carolina severed relations with the United States on May 20, 1861. (NCA.)

Thomas Sloan, pictured in his uniform, enlisted with his brother, George. Thomas served as a musician during the war. He was an accomplished guitar player and drummer. After the war, he returned to Greensboro, worked as a sales clerk, married Mary Gretter, and, after her death, married Mary's sister, Lizzie. (GHMAI.)

Shown is Thomas's drum. The military band served an important role during battle, both lifting morale and alerting the troops. Often the commanding officers could not be heard over the sounds of weapons firing, Rebel yells, and the screams of wounded men, but instruments could. After the battle, in the bivouac, music offered the soldiers a way to express the deep psychological pain suffered during the nightmare of battle. (GHMAI.)

Thomas's brother, George Sloan, died of typhoid in July 1861 at Fort Macon. Disease was the first enemy to besiege the Guilford Grays. Measles, dysentery, typhoid, whooping cough, and other diseases either killed or rendered unfit for service many of the Guilford Grays early in the war. In September 1861, the Guilford Grays become Company B, 27th North Carolina. The Grays remained at Fort Macon (shown) until February 1862. (CAM.)

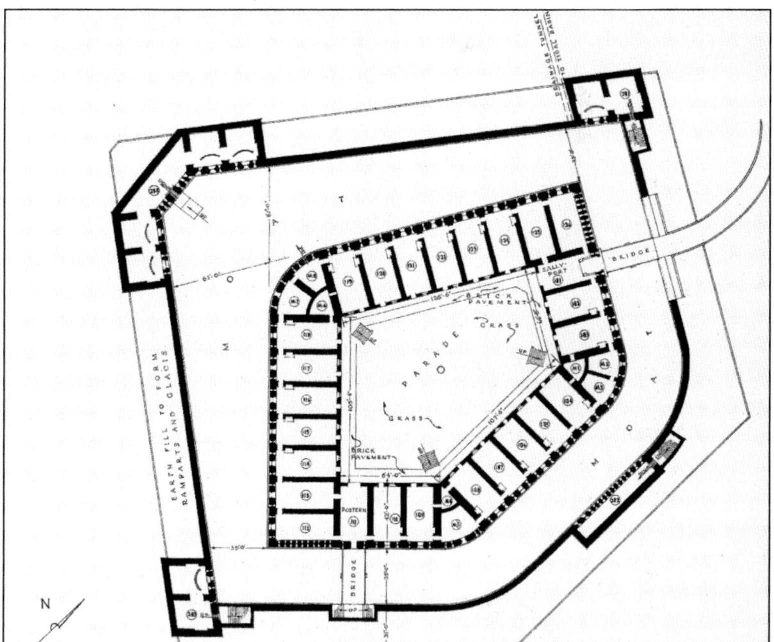

Shown are the casemates of Fort Macon. In casemate 14.5, Harper Lindsay, Ed Higgins, Tom Sloan, Jim Pearce, and J. W. McDowell bunked together. McDowell met his death at Bristow Station, Virginia, in 1863. Lindsay, Higgins, and Sloan joined the regimental band. These men were rowdy, and no one wished to bunk with them. Under the cover of night, they would leave their casemate to visit nearby Beaufort. (LOC.)

A group of women from Beaufort chose to visit the fort to present a flag. An explosion occurred that frightened the men bathing in the surf; they thought the fort was being attacked. The men, naked, ran toward the fort and the unsuspecting women. A woman visiting James T. Morehead nearly suffered an injury when a bomb exploded near her. Shown is a gun at Fort Macon. (CAM.)

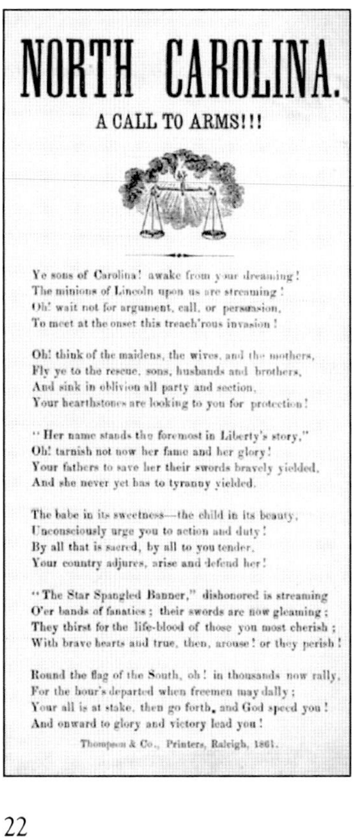

NORTH CAROLINA.

A CALL TO ARMS!!!

Ye sons of Carolina! awake from your dreaming!
The minions of Lincoln upon us are streaming!
Oh! wait not for argument, call, or persuasion,
To meet at the onset this treach'rous invasion!

Oh! think of the maidens, the wives, and the mothers,
Fly ye to the rescue, sons, husbands and brothers,
And sink in oblivion all party and section,
Your hearthstones are looking to you for protection!

"Her name stands the foremost in Liberty's story,"
Oh! tarnish not now her fame and her glory!
Your fathers to save her their swords bravely yielded,
And she never yet has to tyranny yielded.

The babe in its sweetness—the child in its beauty,
Unconsciously urge you to action and duty!
By all that is sacred, by all to you tender,
Your country adjures, arise and defend her!

"The Star Spangled Banner," dishonored is streaming
O'er bands of fanatics; their swords are now gleaming;
They thirst for the life-blood of those you most cherish;
With brave hearts and true, then, arouse! or they perish!

Round the flag of the South, oh! in thousands now rally,
For the hour's departed when freemen may dally;
Your all is at stake, then go forth, and God speed you!
And onward to glory and victory lead you!

Thompson & Co., Printers, Raleigh, 1861.

The Guilford Grays' first battle occurred at New Bern, North Carolina, in March 1862 against troops led by Gen. Ambrose Burnside. S. H. Hunter, struck in the head by a fragment of a shell, died shortly thereafter, the first Guilford Gray casualty. The Grays retreated to Kinston. Shown is a "call of arms" urging all young men to do their duty. (LOC.)

The Confederate States government initiated the Conscription Act in 1862. Confederate president Jefferson Davis (shown) ordered white males between the ages of 18 and 35 to enlist in the Confederate army for three years. The citizens of Greensboro were saddened to hear of the draft; most of their sons had voluntarily enlisted. A few men—doctors, pharmacists, railroad workers, and government leaders—were exempt from active duty. (LOC.)

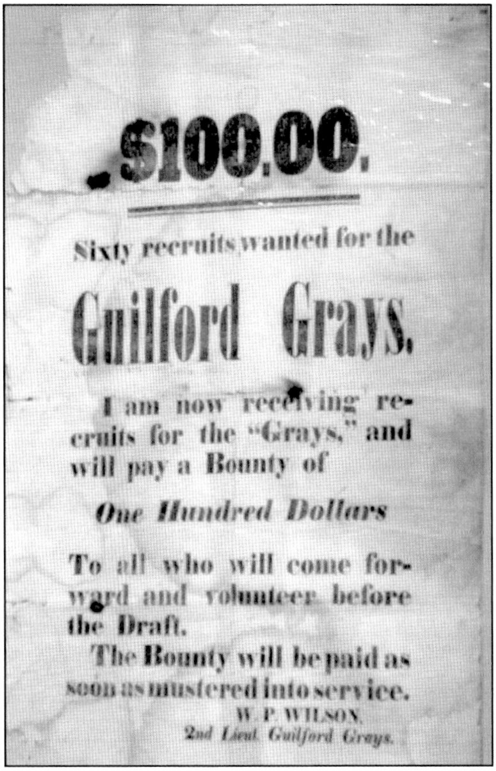

William P. Wilson, a Guilford Gray, offered bounty money to persuade recruits to join the company before the Confederacy drafted them. Wealthy individuals could hire a substitute to go in their place. Jere H. Tarpley provided a substitute and remained in Greensboro, manufacturing guns for the soldiers. Shown is a recruiting banner. (GHMAI.)

Wilson met death not from a bullet but from typhoid disease. Wilson died at his father's home in Greensboro on March 3, 1863. Shown is Wilson's monument in the First Presbyterian Cemetery. Notice the pointed center of the marker. Legend states that the monuments of Confederate soldiers are pointed in the center to make it impossible for Yankees to sit on them. (CAM.)

The Guilford Grays traveled by train to Richmond, Virginia, in the summer of 1862 in time to participate in the Seven Days Battle, which occurred between June 25 and July 1, 1862. Shown is a stereograph of a damaged locomotive in Richmond, the capital of the Confederate States of America. (LOC.)

The Battle of Malvern Hill, Virginia, occurred on July 1, 1862. The Guilford Grays, ordered to advance, faced a blaze of cannon and musket fire. In *Reminiscences of the Guilford Grays*, John A. Sloan states, "Parties from both armies, with lanterns and litters, wandered over the field seeking for the wounded, whose groans could not fail to move with pity the heart of friends and foe." (LOC.)

The Guilford Grays participated in the bombardment of Harper's Ferry, Virginia. Sloan, in *Reminiscences of the Guilford Grays*, relates that "11,000 men surrendered 73 pieces of artillery, 13,000 small arms, and a large quantity of military stores fell into our hands." The Confederate army suffered arms shortages from the onset of the war, often relying on the spoils of battle to replenish their resources. Shown is Harper's Ferry. (LOC.)

Photographer Alexander Gardner created this glass stereograph of Sharpsburg, Maryland, in September 1862. The Guilford Grays, 32 men strong, entered battle at Sharpsburg. William Adams, James E. Edwards, A. F. Coble, James M. Edwards, R. Leyton Smith, R. L. Donnell, W. W. Underwood, and William McFarland died on the field of battle or shortly thereafter. Six wounded men went to the hospital, and several men were taken prisoner. (LOC.)

At Sharpsburg, Maryland, on September 17, 1862, Capt. James Graham recorded, "Forming in a corn-field we advanced under a heavy fire of grape and canister at a quick step up a little rise and halted at a rail fence, our right considerably advanced. After holding this position for half an hour or more our front was changed so as to be on a line with the other troops." (LOC.)

Shown are Confederate dead at Sharpsburg, Maryland. The Guilford Grays won special recognition for boldly standing their ground during the fight without a single bullet. An obituary in the Greensboro *Patriot* reported that Capt. William Adams, fatally wounded in the abdomen, stated, "I am a dead man. Leave me and fight; let me die upon the field." (LOC.)

A Maryland woman prepared Adams's body for burial and cut a lock of his hair to send to his mother as a keepsake. After the war, his remains were retrieved and reburied in Green Hill Cemetery. His parents, Peter and Sarah Adams, are buried nearby. Shown is Adam's final resting place in Greensboro. (CAM.)

The Guilford Grays were out of ammunition. Forced to retreat, they became trapped between enemy forces and prisoners captured earlier in the engagement. The battle of Sharpsburg on September 17, 1862, is known as the bloodiest day of the War Between the States. Shown is a stereograph by Alexander Gardner of the Sunken Road at Sharpsburg, Maryland. (LOC.)

The Grays marched to Fredericksburg, Virginia, in freezing rain and sleet. Their feet, sliced by ice, left bloody footprints on the frozen ground. Their demeanor remained jovial, especially when the troops raided a persimmon tree. Supposedly persimmons could draw a soldier's stomach to the proportions suited to a Confederate ration. Shown is a view of Gen. Ambrose Burnside's Union troops, numbering 100,000, attacking 20,000 Confederate troops. (LOC.)

At the Battle of Fredericksburg, Virginia, on December 13, 1862, Lt. Samuel Weir and Capt. John A. Sloan urged a wounded Col. John A. Gilmer of the 27th North Carolina to leave the battlefield. A Union sharpshooter blasted a lead ball through Weir's temple, killing him instantly. Shown are Cobb's and Kershaw's brigades behind the stone wall at Marye's Heights. (LOC.)

Colonel Gilmer of the 27th North Carolina (shown) refused to leave the theater of battle, demanding that his wounded troops be removed to a place of safety first. The gesture, though noble, probably cost Weir his life. Gilmer recovered from his leg wound in time to engage the enemy in battle at Bristow Station, Virginia, on October 14, 1863. (NCA.)

Sgt. Maj. Robert Dudley Weatherly (shown) received a shell shot that passed through his body and struck Colonel Gilmer. Weatherly was taken to a hospital in Richmond, Virginia. His parents traveled from Greensboro and stayed with their son until he died. They returned to Greensboro with the corpse of their beloved and laid their son to rest in First Presbyterian Cemetery. (EW.)

Gen. Robert E. Lee was beloved by all Confederate soldiers. When questioned about the slaughter after the battle at Bristow Station, he is recorded as saying, "Bury your poor dead, and say nothing more about it." The day after the battle, the Guilford Grays loaded ambulance wagons with wounded men and buried their dead upon the battlefield where they fell. Shown are General Lee and his horse, Traveler. (LOC.)

The Guilford Grays participated in a battle in the Wilderness Campaign on May 5 and 6, 1864, in Virginia. They were in involved in the fighting at Graves' Farm on May 10, 1864, and at Spottsylvania Courthouse on May 12, 1864. Shown is a sketch by Edwin Forbes depicting a battle during the Wilderness Campaign. (LOC.)

Capt. John A. Sloan of the Guilford Grays stated, "We had now completed twelve days of battle at Spotsylvania, and at no time, day or night, did the firing on the lines entirely cease." Shown is Spotsylvania. (LOC.)

This chromolithograph print by Louis Zimmer depicts a Rebel camp. The image shows four African Americans in the camp. African Americans from Greensboro included Jake Mebane (fifer), Bob Hargrove (kettle-drummer), and Caesar Lindsay (base drummer), who all served in the Guilford Gray militia. An African American named Bill, a servant of John A. Sloan, served as Sloan's bodyguard throughout the war. John Gilmer, an African American, was a servant of Col. John Gilmer, a white man. He applied for and received a Confederate pension. (LOC.)

African Americans served as teamsters, cooks, bodyguards, and laborers. Free African Americans received pay for their services. Records of the slaves' plight in Greensboro during the war are scarce. James W. Albright states in *Greensboro 1808–1904*, "It would be unjust to the thousands of slaves in Guilford not to say that they stood by their old owners and their families." Shown are African Americans performing Confederate picket duty in 1863. (LOC.)

At the Second Battle of Cold Harbor, Virginia, on June 4, 1864, ammunition was scarce. The Guilford Grays recruited volunteers to dodge the enemy's bullets to bring back needed ammunition. The Guilford Grays participated in battles at Gary's Farm on June 15, Yellow Tavern on August 21, Ream's Station on August 25, and Bellfield on December 9, totaling 10 major battles in 1864 in Virginia. In 1865, the Grays' first battle of the year was at Hatcher's Run on February 5; then on March 30 at Fort Euliss, Virginia; and on April 2 at Sutherland's Tavern, Virginia. Shown is a stereograph of Cold Harbor taken on June 4, 1864, by Timothy H. O'Sullivan. (LOC.)

Sgt. Daniel W. McConnell, lying in a field hospital located behind the Guilford Grays' line of battle in the trenches at Petersburg, Virginia, suffered paralysis resulting in his death when a bomb exploded near him. Shown is a stereograph image of Petersburg by Timothy H. O'Sullivan. (LOC.)

Shown is a drawing by Alfred R. Waud depicting Petersburg, Virginia, on the morning of July 30, 1864. Guilford Gray captain John A. Sloan explains the events at the crater: "About daylight on the morning of the 30th, this famous mine—afterwards known as the "crater"—was exploded with a great noise, as of a rushing mighty wind, and there was a great earthquake, and the sun became black." (LOC.)

Sloan relates, "Our Company was in line immediately at the crater. In our front and almost under our noses, lay the bloated, festering bodies of their dead, exposed to the scorching rays of a July sun." The Guilford Grays stayed in and around the trenches until September 1864. Shown is a drawing by Alfred R. Waud of a scene in the trenches at Petersburg in September 1864. (LOC.)

At Appomattox, Virginia, on April 9, 1865, only 12 men of the Guilford Grays answered roll call. Silas Carter Dodson, shown, was one of them. After the war, he worked for the Richmond and Danville Railroad. In 1877, he served Greensboro as mayor. He died on June 24, 1906. (EB.)

A horse kicked Jed Harper Lindsay Jr. on the first day of fighting at Gettysburg. He returned to Greensboro, maintained a supportive role while recovering from his injury, and returned to duty. He surrendered at Appomattox on April 9, 1865. In addition to bullets and disease, accidents rendered many soldiers unfit for combat duty. (UNCH.)

(Confederate.)

S | 27 | N. C.

John A Sloan ×

Capt, Co. B, 27 North Carolina Reg't.

Appears on a

List

of Prisoners of War belonging to the Army of Northern Virginia, who have been this day surrendered by General Robert E. Lee, C. S. A., commanding said Army, to Lieut. Genl. U. S. Grant, commanding Armies of the United States.

Done at Appomattox Court House, Virginia, April 9, 1865.

List dated Not dated

Remarks: 1 private horse, side arms & clothing

Capt. John A. Sloan stated in his book, *Reminiscences of the Guilford Grays*, what he saw upon his arrival home. "After four long years, we returned to our homes in tattered and battle-stained garments, footsore, weary, and with aching hearts. We returned to see poverty, desolation, and ruin; to find the hearts of our loved ones buried in the graves of the dead Confederacy." Sloan was allowed to keep his horse, clothes, and sidearms. (NA.)

Three

COMRADES IN ARMS

Capt. John Austin Lindsay (shown), a member of the North State Boys, Company K, 45th North Carolina, was wounded in the left foot at Gettysburg, Pennsylvania, on July 1, 1863, and lost his ability to march long distances. Lindsay states, "I cannot walk any great distances, it being on account of the weakness of my foot, impossible for me to walk half a mile without great suffering . . . yet I am willing to do all that is in my power to keep this country from being overrun by the detestable Yankees." (UNCH.)

Lindsay was retired to the invalid corps, a group of sick and injured men unfit for actual combat but capable of performing supportive tasks. Early in the war, unfit combatants were discharged, but the need for soldiers greatly increased as the years of war took their toll on eligible young men. The invalid corps was created as a support group. Shown is Lindsay's sister, Charlotte. (UNCH.)

Lindsay was a son of Robert and Marianna Perry Austin Lindsay of Greensboro. The Lindsays, though heartbroken to learn their son was wounded, were probably elated to have him back home with them during the turbulent years of war. Shown is Lindsay's brother-in-law, Alexander M. Peyton. The *carte de visite* became popular during the War Between the States. A Mr. Bendann, a photographer in Maryland, created this particular card before 1878. (UNCH.)

Col. John Henry Morehead of the 45th North Carolina (shown), sickened with typhoid fever, fought his private war against a killer disease and lost. He traveled by horseback, attempting to reach Greensboro, when his diseased body could go no farther. Morehead died on June 26, 1863. Good Samaritans cared for him like a son. When he died, he received a Christian burial while his beloved wife, Susan, and daughter, Minnie, in Greensboro hopelessly waited for him to return home. After the war, his funeral was held in the Old Methodist Church in Greensboro, and his remains were reburied in the First Presbyterian Cemetery. Disease was the primary killer of Greensboro's Confederate soldiers. (UNCH.)

Charles Webster Woollen was a merchant in Greensboro at the time he entered the service of the Confederate army. A soldier of the Company B, 45th North Carolina, Woollen's killer was typhoid fever. He died in Richmond, Virginia, on July 4, 1863. Shown is his final resting place in Green Hill Cemetery. (CAM.)

Lt. S. Washington Donnell enlisted in Greensboro in the Guilford Light Infantry, Company C, 45th North Carolina. Born in 1844, he died in battle at Fisher's Hill near Strasburg, Virginia, on September 22, 1864. His body was returned home for burial in Greensboro's Buffalo Presbyterian Cemetery. In the early 21st century, grave robbers violated his grave when they attempted to dig up his earthly remains. Shown is Donnell's gravestone. (CAM.)

The Confederate army consisted of men from all ranks of life and occupations. Before enlisting in the Company B, 45th North Carolina, Capt. Samuel C. Rankin taught school. At Gettysburg, Rankin received an injury to his foot, enabling the enemy to take him prisoner. He would spend the next 20 months in a Federal prison at Johnson's Island in Sandusky, Ohio. Pictured from left to right are Rankin, J. A. (John) Roach, and C. B. (Cyrus) Watson. (CLARK.)

The 45th North Carolina endured deadly artillery fire, suffering greatly, but succeeded in charging the enemy forces at Gettysburg. (CAM.)

Shown from left to right are the Norman brothers: (first row) Lacy J., M. T., and William M.; (second row) Frederick W., Matthew H., and Jackson. M. T. served in the 37th Battalion Virginia Cavalry (Dunn's Battalion Partisan Rangers). Capt. Lacy J. Norman, Company B, 2nd Battalion North Carolina Infantry, was wounded at Gettysburg, Pennsylvania, and Cedar Creek, Virginia. He received his parole in Richmond, Virginia, in May 1865. Lt. Mathew H. Norman, Company A, 28th North Carolina, was captured in 1863 and spent the rest of the war in prison at Johnson's Island with his brother William M., Company A, 2nd North Carolina. William M. wrote a diary during his imprisonment entitled *A Portion of My Life*. Many families offered more than one son for military service. (MNM.)

William M. Norman's original diary contains the signatures of prisoners held with him at Johnson's Island. Capt. Pleasant A. Tatum, Company F, 2nd North Carolina Cavalry from Greensboro, was one of Norman's roommates and regularly dined with him. Lt. Col. William S. Rankin of the 21st North Carolina, a former captain of the Guilford Dixie Boys from Greensboro, resided in the same block as Norman. Early in their imprisonment food was plentiful, but in the final days, men suffered starvation. Shown is Norman. (MNM.)

Remembrances from loved ones at home gave comfort to the prisoners. Norman recalled the pleasant gifts of food and clothes his "affectionate wife" sent him. Norman's diary, a record of his military experiences, is also a beautiful love story honoring his wife and little daughter. Shown is Letitia Holyfield Norman, his wife. (MNM.)

Norman arrived home starved and in poor health. The brutal northern winters waged another kind of war on Confederate prisoners. The men suffered greatly, particularly after rumors spread that Northern prisoners were starving and suffering atrocities in Southern prisons. The small boy sitting on the ground is Romie Snow. From left to right are (first row) William M. Norman, Letitia H. Norman, John Holyfield, Jimmy Holyfield, Emma Norman Holyfield, Watson Norman, Almedia Casstevens Norman, Percy Norman, Rosa Norman Hicks, and Lettie Bet Norman; (second row) Titia May Norman, Lacy Norman, Hardin Norman, Ray Norman, Ellen N. Bass, Rush Norman, Ada Holyfield Loflin, George Matthews, and Paulina Norman Mathews. (MNM.)

Shown are Norman and fellow comrades in arms of the 2nd North Carolina. At center is Col. William R. Cox; clockwise from top are Col. John P. Cobb; surgeon George L. Kirby; Capt. W. T. Faircloth; Capt. William M. Norman, Company A; Maj. D. W. Hurtt; and Col. Charles C. Tew. Company E consisted of 125 men from Guilford County. The remaining regiments hailed from Sampson, Surry, Wilson, Wayne, New Hanover, Craven, Jones, and Pamlico Counties in North Carolina. (CLARK.)

Second Lt. Joseph Motley Morehead, Company E, 2nd North Carolina, also known as the Guilford Guards, enlisted with the company in Greensboro in July 1861. He resigned due to a spinal problem in January 1862. He was a former Guilford Gray. Many men were physically incapable of withstanding the harsh military conditions demanded of them. (CALD.)

Shown around 1896 is the Clapp family home located in eastern Guilford County. The men on the porch are unknown. From left to right are Lemuel Clapp, Sally Flack, Novel McKean, Eli Ernest, Eli Peter Rankin, Floyd Dowie, Rosa Bell Brown, Annie Rena, Rosina A. Helen, William L. Monroe, Ella Clapp, and Emma Ada Clapp. Lemuel served in Company F, 54th North Carolina. He was wounded in the face at Hatcher's Run, Virginia, in February 1865. As the war progressed, families suffered greatly from shortages and concern for their loved ones. (JR.)

Shown is the Clapp family, from left to right: (first row) Sally Flack, Lemuel Clapp, Floyd Dowie, Rosa Belle Brown, Eli Peter Rankin, Eli Ernest, and Annie Rena Clapp; (second row) Anna Rena Ella, William L. Monroe, Emma Ada S., Rosina A., and Novel McKean Clapp. Lemuel received his parole in Greensboro on May 11, 1865. Eli Peter Rankin Clapp, born in 1861, appears to be named in honor of brothers Eli Peter and Peter Rankin Clapp of the Guilford Dixie Boys, who died in 1861 of typhoid. (JR.)

Brig. Gen. Alfred Moore Scales (1827–1892) enlisted as a private in Company H, 13th North Carolina. He quickly advanced in rank. He was wounded in the thigh at Chancellorsville in May 1863. Scales said, "That third day of May, 1863, at Chancellorsville, was one that tried men's souls." The 13th North Carolina lost 203 men in the engagement. Scales is shown in his uniform in this tintype. (LOC.)

Scales (shown) stated, "If I must shed my blood in battle, I will shed it for the South and my people and not against them." Many of the young men in Greensboro shared the same sentiment. Scales served in the House of Commons and was elected governor of North Carolina in 1884. He resided in Greensboro and was one of Greensboro's most beloved citizens. (UNC.)

Col. Junius Irving Scales (1832–1880) moved to Carrollton, Mississippi, shortly before the War Between the States with his bride, Effie Hamilton Henderson, with whom he eventually had eight children. He enlisted in the 30th Mississippi and was taken prisoner at Chickamauga in 1863, spending the rest of the war incarcerated at Johnson's Island. After the war, he moved to Greensboro. (CALD.)

Lt. Col. Alexander C. McAllister, 46th North Carolina, was one of the fortunate soldiers to survive the brutality of war. He received his parole on May 1, 1865, in Greensboro. Shown in the center is Col. William L. Saunders; clockwise from top are Lt. Col. Alexander C. McAllister, Capt. Robert Preston Troy, Capt. Obed William Carr, Capt. Adolphus Theodrose Bost, Capt. Jesse Franklin Heflin, and Capt. Robert A. Bost. (CLARK.)

Charles M. Stedman (shown) volunteered as a private in the Fayetteville Independent Light Infantry. He was wounded at Bethel on June 10, 1861, but survived, reached the rank of major of the 44th North Carolina, and surrendered with General Lee at Appomattox in 1865. Stedman moved to Greensboro in 1898 and was active in his law career, serving as president of the North Carolina Bar Association. He also served in the congress of the United States. (NCMA.)

Lt. Col. Christopher Columbus Cole (shown) began his military career as a member of the Guilford Men, Company E, 22nd North Carolina. The Guilford Men enlisted in Greensboro on May 23, 1861. Printed in the *Patriot* newspaper in 1868, one of Cole's diary entries described a battle: "he could see a blue canvas above him made of the whirring bullets, and the thick dust which was knocked up, almost suffocated the men." (EB.)

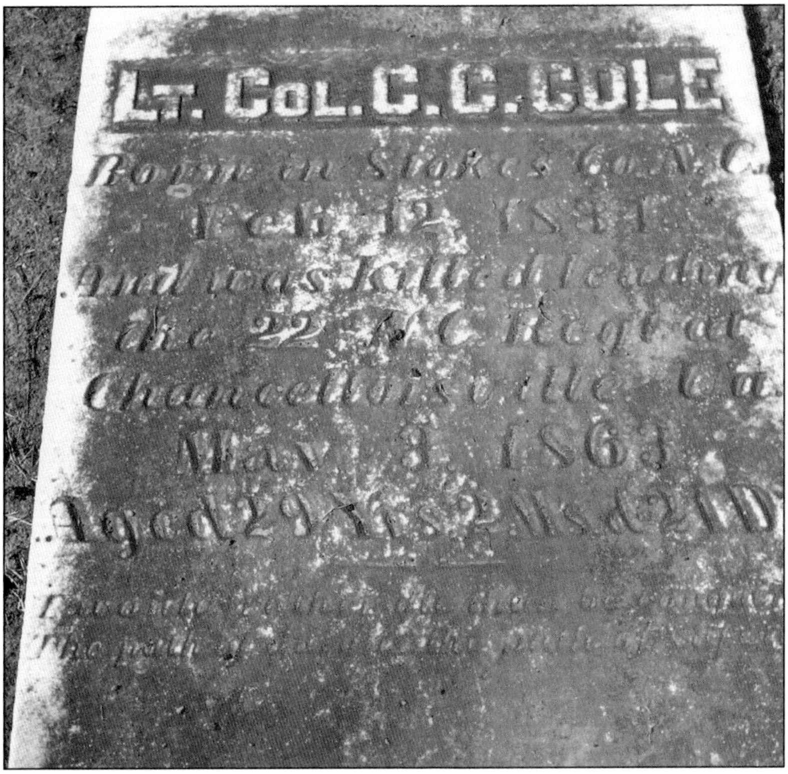

Christopher's brother, James Cole, served as adjutant of the 22nd North Carolina. One evening in the Shenandoah Valley, the two brothers sat in front of the campfire reminiscing—a rare moment because James resigned due to consumption in February 1863 and Christopher met death at Chancellorsville, Virginia on May 3, 1863. Cole was buried in the Old Methodist Cemetery; his grave marker is in Green Hill Cemetery. (CAM.)

Washington C. Orrell was more fortunate that Cole. Though he was wounded in the thigh at Ream's Station, Virginia, he survived the war. Orrell's brothers, Aseph, James, and Daniel, served in the Confederate army. The men from Greensboro and Guilford County shared kinship, friendship, and a deep love for their homeland. Shown is Orrell's monument in Green Hill Cemetery. (CAM.)

John A. Swain from neighboring Alamance County, enlisted in the 47th North Carolina. Though he was shot twice in battle, he survived to surrender in Greensboro in May 1865. His monument is a government-issued marker in Green Hill Cemetery. The symbol carved on the marker is the Southern Cross of Honor. Swain and his comrade, Washington C. Orrell, joined the United Confederate Veterans upon its establishment in Greensboro in 1896. (CAM.)

Four

Greensboro's Elite

Dr. James King Hall's resignation from the Confederate army read, "Sir, I have the honor to tender the resignation of my appointment as surgeon of the 22nd Regiment North Carolina Troops which I respectfully ask you to consider and forward to the proper authority and which I hope will be accepted. In asking this favor, I would state that I am forty-five years of age and feel that my health will not justify my remaining longer in so active service with justice to myself or my regiment. . . . Respectfully your Obedient Servant, J. K. Hall." Hall was released from military duty. He served as president of the North Carolina Medical Society in 1883. (GHMAI.)

North Carolina Senators and Repres
Confederate Con
Senator Wm.W.Avery
July 2o,1861-Feb.17,1862
Burke County.
Representative H. R. Bridgers
Feb. 18,1862-Mar. 18,1865
Second District
Edgecombe County
Representative Burton Craige
July 23,1861-Feb. 18,1862
Honorable Jefferson Davis
President of the Confederate States,
1861-1865.
Representative O. R. Kenan
Feb. 18,1862-Feb. 17,1864
Third District
Duplin County
Representative William Lander
Feb. 18,1862-Feb. 17,1864
Eighth District
Lincoln County.
Representative J. M. Leach
Seventh District
Davidson County
Representative J. M. Morehead
July 20,1861-Feb. 18,1862
Fifth District
Guilford County
Representative R. C. Puryear
July 20,1861-Feb. 18, 1862
Sixth District
Surry County
Representative J. G. Ramsay
May 2,1864-Mar. 18,1865
Eighth District
Rowan County.
Representative Thomas Ruffin

Members of the Confederate Congress pictured in this image are, from left to right, (first row) J. M. Morehead, R. C. Puryear, J. G. Ramsay, Thomas Ruffin, W. N. H. Smith, Josiah Turner, and A. W. Venable; (second row) O. R. Kenan, William Lander, J. W. Leach, J. T. Leach, T. D. S. McDowell, G. W. Logan, and J. R. McLean; (third row) H. R. Brigders, Burton Craige, A. T. Davidson, Pres. Jefferson Davis, T. C. Fuller, B. S. Gaither, and J. A. Gilmer; (fourth row) William W. Avery, George Davis, William T. Dorich, William A. Graham, E. G. Reade, A. H. Arrington, and T. S. Ashe. John Adams Gilmer, James Robert McLean, and John Motley Morehead, Confederate Congress representatives from Guilford County, resided in Greensboro. (UNC.)

James Turner Morehead, son of John Motley and Ann Eliza Lindsay Morehead, served in the 63rd North Carolina. Shot through the mouth during battle, he was sent home and considered an invalid but miraculously survived his wound and the war. (UNC.)

Morehead's brother-in-law, Peter Gustavous Evans of the 63rd North Carolina, was not as lucky as Morehead. Shot mortally at the Battle of Upperville, Virginia, Evans was captured and taken to Washington City for medical treatment by the Yankees. Upon his death, he was buried there. After the war, his remains were disinterred and taken to Greensboro for reburial in the Evans family plot in First Presbyterian Cemetery. (CLARK.)

Jesse Rankin Wharton (1833–1904), the son of Watson and Malinda Wharton, settled his wife, Mattie Turner, and their children safely at his parents' home and enlisted in the 12th Battalion Virginia Artillery with his friend James W. Albright. Friends and family members often enlisted together. Though he was a farmer, he had a passion for education. After the war, he served as a superintendent of Guilford County's schools. Wharton is shown here. (CALD.)

Lt. Col. William Lafayette Scott of the 21st North Carolina enlisted in June 1861 in Company M, the Guilford Dixie Boys, consisting primarily of men from Greensboro and Guilford County. The Guilford Dixie Boys was the second company organized in the community for service in the Confederate army. By 1862, Scott felt the war was a lost cause and advocated peace. Many people in Greensboro resented his peace efforts and labeled him a coward. (GHMAI.)

In a letter written at Morton's Ferry dated December 7, 1863, Dr. John Early Logan, surgeon for the 14th North Carolina, spoke of having dinner with Harper Lindsay. He relates that the box of onions, sweet potatoes, and ketchup sent from home were a special treat. In another letter he relates, "Do you know anybody who wants to be my sweetheart long enough to knit me a pair of gloves? Am sadly in need of something of the sort (I mean gloves). Of all my sweethearts, not one thinks enough of me to knit me a pair of gloves. All the dear little creatures have lost their patriotism." Shown is Harper Lindsay, a member of the 27th North Carolina. (UNCG.)

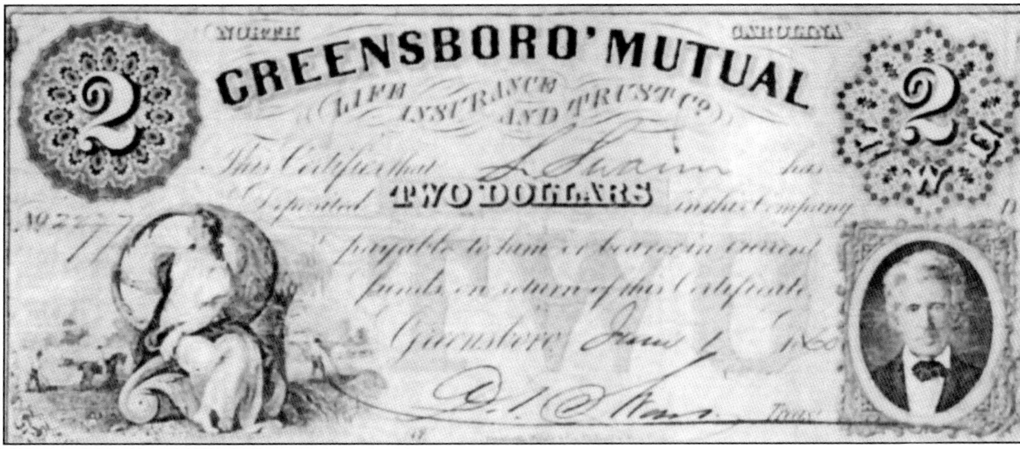

Shown is a $2 note payable to L. Swaim. The Greensboro Mutual Life Insurance and Trust Company produced 25¢ and 50¢ paper money printed on wallpaper during the war until it went bankrupt. Logan often wrote his brother-in-law, Lyndon Swaim, requesting money. He asked his sister to remember him in her daily devotions. (CAM.)

Dr. John Early Logan surrendered at Appomattox, returned to Greensboro, and continued his medical practice and business pursuits. He and his wife, Fannie Sloan, donated large sums of money to aid a medical facility in Greensboro. Pharmacists and physicians pictured with Logan are (center) W. C. Porter; (clockwise from top) Dr. James King Hall, Dr. ? Beall, Dr. ? Micnaux, William S. Porter (O. Henry), and Dr. ? Wilson. (CALD.)

Maj. Joseph Motley Morehead (1840–1911), the son of James Turner Morehead, a member of the Eclectic Club, took an interest in providing a final resting place for the dead Confederate soldiers buried in trench graves in the Greensboro area. He was active in promoting the Guilford Battleground as a national park. This postcard depicts the Guilford Battleground and Morehead. (CAM.)

Joseph's brother, Col. James Turner Morehead, wrote a sketch of the 53rd North Carolina, published in *Clark's Regiments*, in which he said, "The characteristics of this regiment were common to North Carolina troops. Obedience to and reverence for law and authority, for which the State has been so long known, in my opinion, constitute the basis of soldierly qualities for which her soldiers will be famous in history." (CALD.)

Shown is James's insignia from his military service. The initials GG signify the Guilford Grays; the stars represent his rank in the 53rd North Carolina. After the war, he returned to Greensboro and his legal practice. James wrote, "Peace hath her victories no less renowned than war." He surrendered at Appomattox. (GHMAI.)

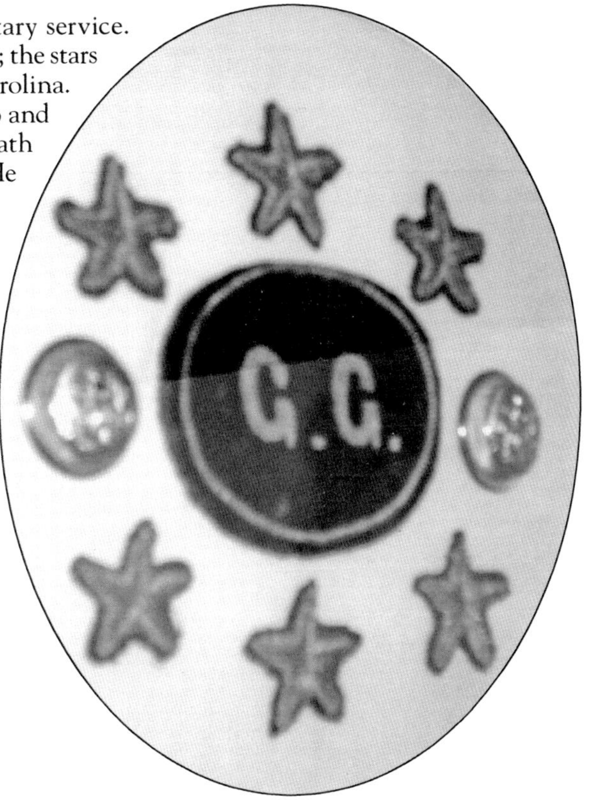

Ralph Gorrell (shown), a Greensboro attorney, managed funds for the Confederate States Treasury locally. His son Henry was shot to death, and his son Julius died from disease during the War Between the States, devastating Gorrell. At the close of the war, his home sheltered leaders of North Carolina and the Confederacy. (CALD.)

Jesse H. Lindsay (shown), a leading banker in Greensboro, became concerned about his bank's assets when turmoil exploded in Greensboro at the close of the war. He asked John C. Wharton to hide the bank's funds. (CALD.)

John C. Wharton (shown) buried the money, silver, and gold on his farm, placed a pigpen upon it, and hid the loot until it was safe to return the valuables to the bank. Rumors persist in Greensboro that lost Confederate treasure is buried in Greensboro and the surrounding community that has never been found. Wharton was a member of the home guard. (CALD.)

Jed H. Lindsay, Jesse's brother, was a leader in Greensboro and a member of the home guard. Jed lost a son, R. Henry Lindsay, in the early days of the war. His son Thomas served in a North Carolina regiment that merged with a Georgia regiment. During the latter part of the war, available human resources were exhausted to the point that it was difficult to fill the shrinking regiments. (CALD.)

Shown is a requisition order signed by J. H. Lindsay, a son of Jed Harper Lindsay and his namesake. Notice that the letter "C" overwrites the letter "U" in U.S. Army. The Confederate army suffered shortages and utilized material belonging to the United States at every opportunity. J. H. Lindsay surrendered at Appomattox, Virginia, in April 1865. (NA.)

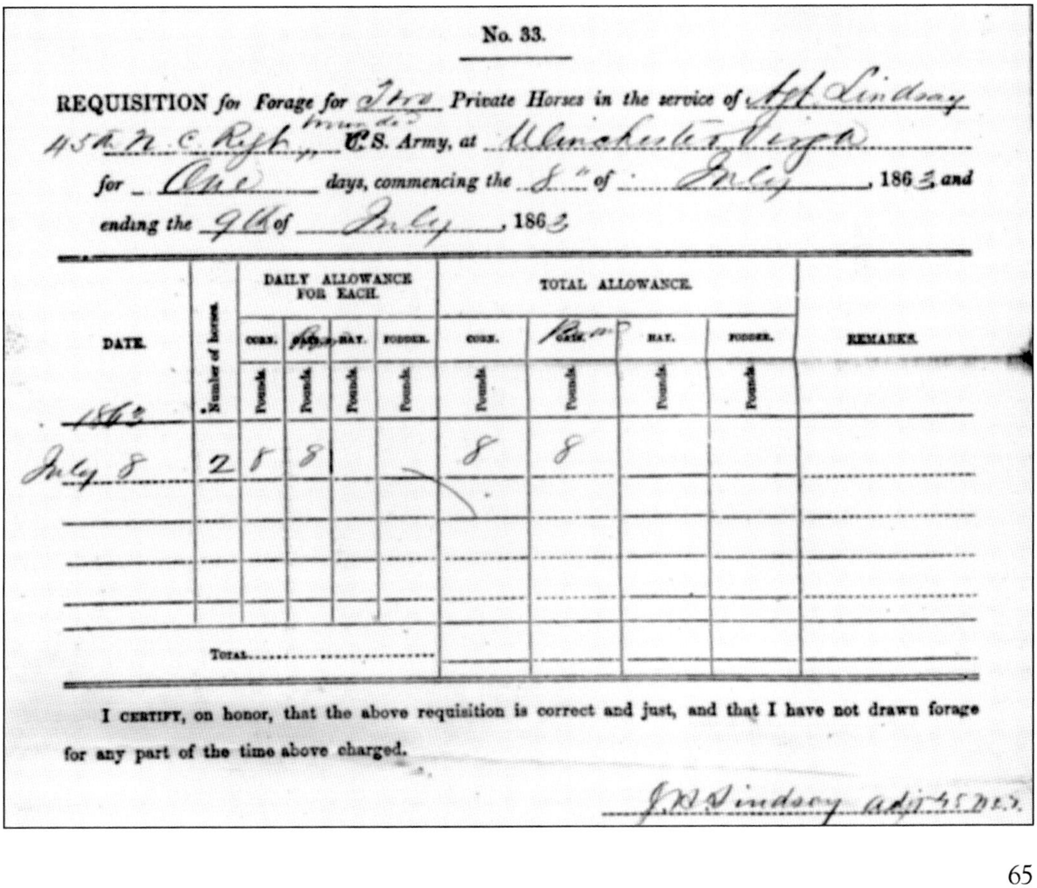

No. 33.

REQUISITION *for Forage for* Two *Private Horses in the service of* Adjt Lindsay 45th N. C. Regt mounted C.S. *Army, at* Winchester Virga *for* One *days, commencing the* 8th *of* July *, 186*3 *and ending the* 9th *of* July *, 186*3

DATE.	Number of horses.	DAILY ALLOWANCE FOR EACH. Corn. Pounds.	Bran (Oats.) Pounds.	Hay. Pounds.	Fodder. Pounds.	TOTAL ALLOWANCE. Corn. Pounds.	Bran (Oats.) Pounds.	Hay. Pounds.	Fodder. Pounds.	REMARKS.
1863										
July 8	2	8	8			8	8			
TOTAL										

I CERTIFY, on honor, that the above requisition is correct and just, and that I have not drawn forage for any part of the time above charged.

J. H. Lindsay Adjt 45 N.C.T.

J. W. Scott, Company A, 53rd North Carolina was taken prisoner in 1864 in Winchester, Virginia. He was incarcerated at Fort Delaware. After the war, he worked as a clerk before creating his own business, J. W. Scott and Company. Shown from left to right are (seated) J. W. Scott, David Schenck, and D. W. C. Benbow; (standing) Julius A. Gray and T. B. Keogh, all members of the Guilford Battleground Company. (NCMA.)

Scott's business specialized in wholesale and retail goods, notions, and groceries. Shown is J. W. Scott's grave marker in Green Hill Cemetery. (CAM.)

Five

SOLDIERS' AID

The women of Greensboro actively supported the young men from their community and throughout the South, beginning with the presentation of swords by the young women of Greensboro Female College and the flag presentation by the young girls of Edgeworth Female Seminary. The women saved every scrap of material and food, and creatively developed food substitutions to keep their families from starving. The supporting role continued, though by the last days of war, the women found themselves engaged in physical combat with their own army for lifesaving food stored in the commissaries in Greensboro. Shown is an illustration published in *Frank Leslie's Illustrated Newspaper* on May 23, 1863. (LOC.)

Susan Dick Weir Bell, a member of the Soldier's Aid Society established in Greensboro at the onset of the war, worked diligently with the women of Greensboro to meet the needs of the young soldiers. Sewing groups met regularly; the spinning wheel was put to use. Every scrap of material was saved for the Southern cause. The women of Greensboro proudly wore old clothes and homespun, not daring to waste one shred of material. Shortly after the Battle of Fredericksburg, on December 13, 1862, Susan received a telegraph informing her of the death of her beloved stepson, Samuel Weir. After the surrender of the Confederate army, she actively promoted social events to entertain the Yankee soldiers. As a former teacher and artist, she designed elaborate ball gowns out of curtains for the young women of Greensboro. (GHMAI.)

Shown is the Weir home. The house provided shelter to refugees fleeing the war from the eastern portions of North Carolina. Decades after the war, the old house sheltered members of the Weir, Rankin, and Dick families, as well as former slaves of the families. The house, located on Edgeworth Street, is currently the home of the Greensboro's Women's Club. It is on the National Register of Historic Places. (CAM.)

The Soldier's Aid Society of Greensboro sent the 22nd North Carolina bed ticks, feather pillows and cases, sheets, comforts, and towels for use in their field hospital. Herbs, alcohol, and medicine were sent to aid the soldiers. The women held sales at Yates Hall to raise funds to purchase supplies for the soldiers. Shown is Agnes Long, the wife of James Long. She was a member of the Soldier's Aid Society and died in 1864 from consumption. (LONG.)

Shown is Mary Eloise Dick, a member of the Soldier's Aid Society who helped prepare packages throughout the war to ease the suffering of the soldiers. Food items such as vinegar, red pepper, rice, sugar, tomatoes, ketchup, dried apples, peaches, blackberries, pickles, butter, honey, mutton suet, and tea were sent. Alcoholic beverages consisting of blackberry wine and peach brandy were sent in the hopes of aiding suffering soldiers. (GHMAI.)

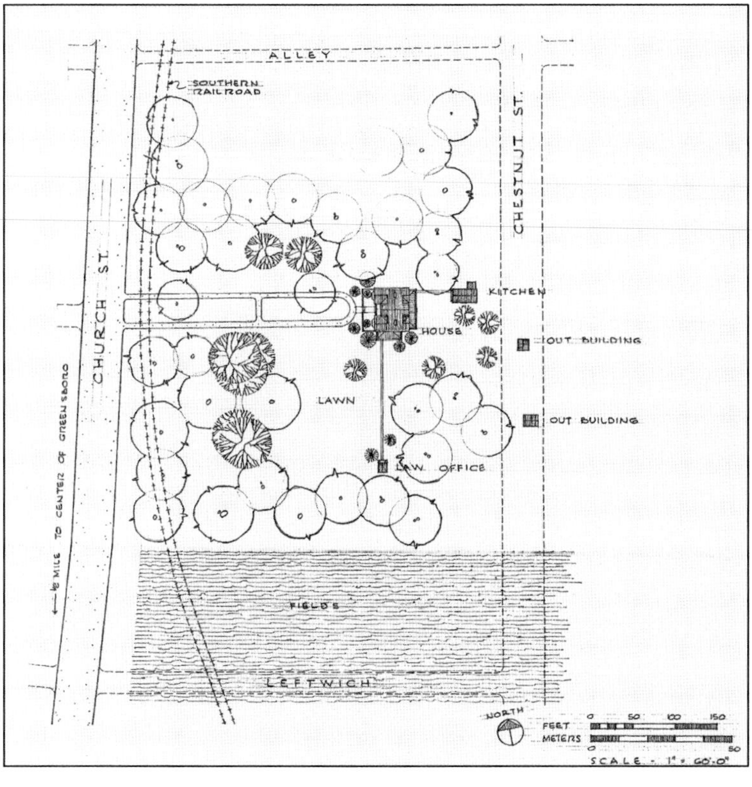

Shown is a blueprint of Dick's home, Dunleath. In 1865, Union general Jacob Cox commandeered the home as his headquarters, forcing the Dick family to reside in the outbuildings. The U.S. flag was flown on the grounds. Appalled, the family avoided walking under the flag. Train tracks located near the house were a main avenue for transporting troops and supplies during the latter part of the war. (LOC.)

The women organized in shifts to be available at a moment's notice to meet the needs of soldiers passing through Greensboro en route to battlefields as well as the wounded and sick men returning from battle. The years of war took their toll on the resources of the women. They too deserve honor for their sacrifices; though they did not wear the uniform of the soldier, their support system and their sufferings qualify them as Confederate soldiers from Greensboro. The war years took their toll on the women; black mourning dress became the fashion of the day. Shown are members of the Sloan family, from left to right: (first row) Ida Louise Sloan Ellington, Fannie Logan, Robert Moderwell Sloan, and Julia Sloan Mebane; (second row) Roberta Porter, Mattie Barringer, and Virginia Sloan Scales. (GHMAI.)

Shown is a drawing by Alfred Rudolph Waud depicting the first day of fighting at Bentonville on March 19, 1865. After the Battle of Bentonville, hundreds of sick and wounded soldiers arrived in Greensboro in need of care. Churches, schools, private homes, and the courthouse quickly became hospitals. The Soldier's Aid Society attempted to ease the great suffering of these men while trying to maintain their homes with enough food and supplies. They made do with substitutes for coffee and sugar, and wore homespun clothes. (LOC.)

Items to enhance the personal comfort of the soldiers such as socks, shirts, boots, coats, books, newspapers, and religious tracts were sent to needy soldiers. Shown is Frances Webb Bumpass, publisher of the *Weekly Message*, who managed to keep her press running throughout the war. She shared her food with passing soldiers. When enemy soldiers camped in her yard, she invited them to join in Christian worship with her. (CALD.)

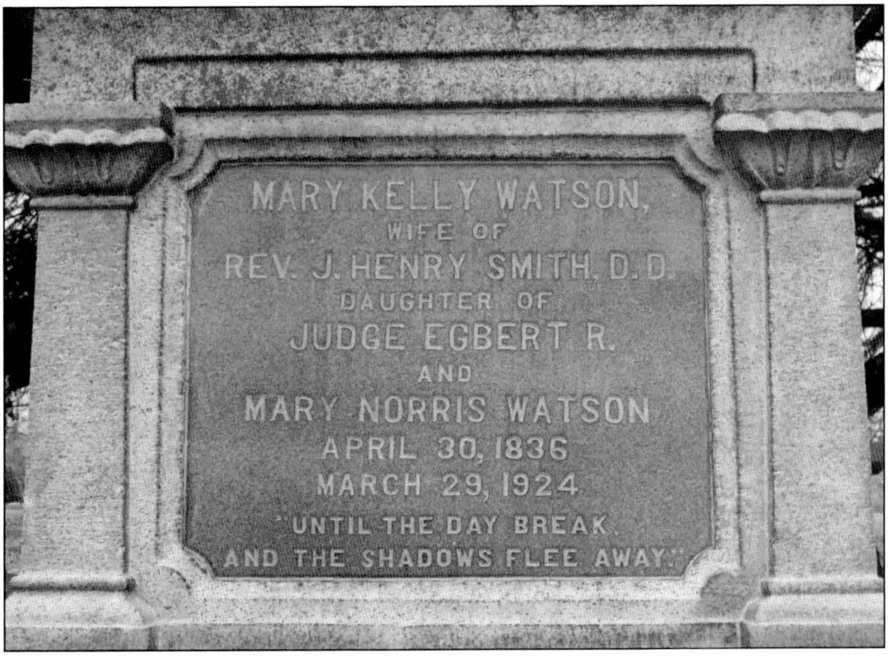

Mary Watson Smith recorded in her diary the effects of the War Between the States on the citizens of Greensboro. She also wrote an article entitled *Women of Greensboro* that told of "the heartache that never lifted" from the bosoms of women in Greensboro during the long war years. Shown is Smith's monument. (GHMAI.)

Rev. Jacob Henry Smith visited and preached to the Confederate military during the war. His brother Charles died while in the service of the Confederate army; his brother Alphonso suffered a fatal wound on June 9, 1862. Smith and his congregation removed the church bell and offered it and the church building to the Confederate government. During the occupation of Greensboro, he preached to both Union and Confederate soldiers. (JW.)

In 1865, the First Presbyterian Church building (shown) served as a field hospital. Mary Watson Smith remembered, "That night in the old Presbyterian church and lecture room, I saw the first wounded and dying men, and witnessed the grief of their comrades. When I went back next morning, death had set its seal on many a noble form that day in a semi-circle around the pulpit." (SIMP.)

The war dead were laid in a row in the back of the churchyard for burial. It is not known if their burials occurred in the churchyard permanently or if their remains were laid there temporarily and removed later. In 1869, the women of Greensboro took a leading role in providing the war dead with a decent burial. Shown is the cemetery. (CAM.)

Bullets from Union and Confederate soldiers, excavated in the cemetery in 2007, lend credibility to the scant historical research indicating that both Union and Confederate soldiers occupied the grounds. Once the Federal troops occupied Greensboro, the wounded men in the church building moved to Edgeworth Female Seminary. (KEITH.)

Edgeworth Female Seminary, shown, served as a field hospital during the war. Soldiers were dying within its walls by 1861. In 1865, Yankee soldiers set up camp on the campus grounds. (GHMAI.)

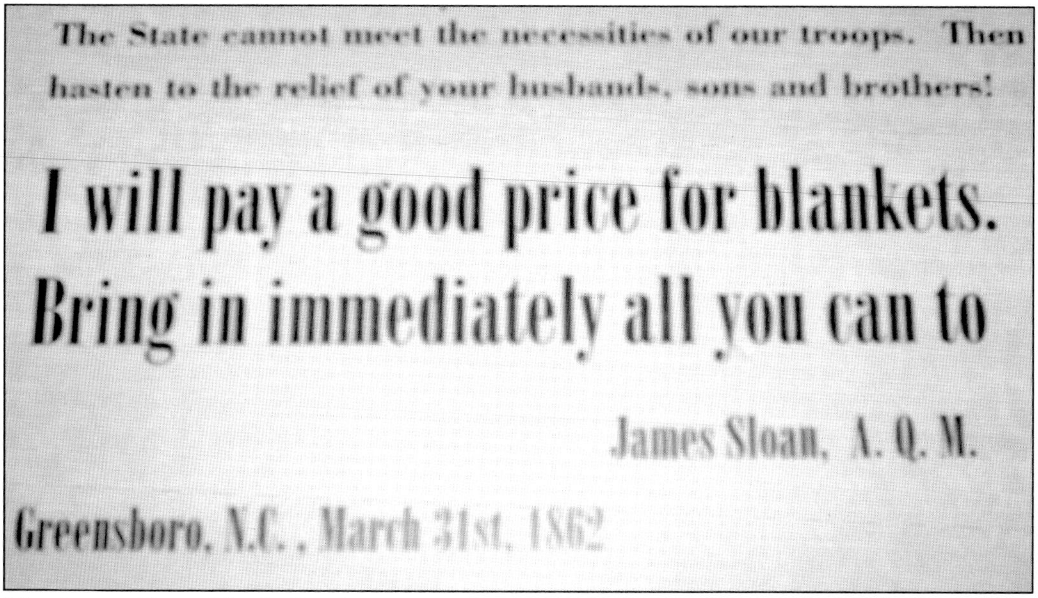

Maj. James Sloan, North Carolina state quartermaster during the war, actively attempted to provide for the soldiers. Shown is an advertisement pleading for the people of Greensboro to bring blankets for their husbands, sons, and brothers. The advertisement, dated 1862, offered payment for goods. (GHMAI.)

Arthur P. Ford, shown, wrote in his book *Life in the Confederate Army and Some Experiences and Sketches*, "At Greensboro, the courthouse was used as the hospital, all the benches, desks, etc, being removed. We had no mattresses, nor bedding of any kind, and about 200 of us were laid off in rows on the floor, with only our blankets that we brought with us. After looking over the accommodations, I selected the platform inside of the rail, where the judge's desk used to be, for my place, and went out into the street and begged an armful of hay from a wagon, and with two bricks for a pillow made my bed. Here I lay for about three weeks with fever and at times very ill. Three times a day the ladies of the town came and brought us food, and were devoted in their attentions." (DOC.)

Ford, very sick, departed the courthouse, made it home to South Carolina, and survived the war. He relates that his health improved once he left the confines of the courthouse. The postcard depicts the courthouse in Greensboro, similar in style to the courthouse that was used as a hospital and burned down after the war. The women of Greensboro adopted all soldiers that passed through Greensboro. (CAM.)

During the war, Ruth Worth Porter assisted her son, Dr. Algernon Sidney Porter, treating wounded soldiers. During the occupation of Greensboro by Federal troops, the soldiers favored her yard. They enjoyed her well water and the greens that grew wild in her yard. The Porters had a relative serving in the Union army that was encamped at Edgeworth Female Seminary. Many families had relatives soldiering in opposing armies. (GHMAI.)

Evelina Maria Porter, known as "Miss Lina," was the daughter of Ruth Worth Porter. She watched helplessly as her sickly brother, Charles E. Porter (1839–1865), enlisted in the Guilford Grays. Some Porter family members were exempt from military service because of their occupations as doctors and pharmacists, a valuable asset on the home front. Evelina was an aunt of William Sydney Porter, better known in the literary world as O. Henry. (GHMAI.)

Shown is Anna Eliza Morehead Evans, daughter of John Motley Morehead. She shared the same fate as many young wives during the War Between the States: she was widowed in 1863. Her husband's comrades wrote to her to extend their heartfelt sympathy, as was common upon the death of a soldier. Some time after the war, her husband's remains were returned to Greensboro for burial in the Evans family plot. (PG.)

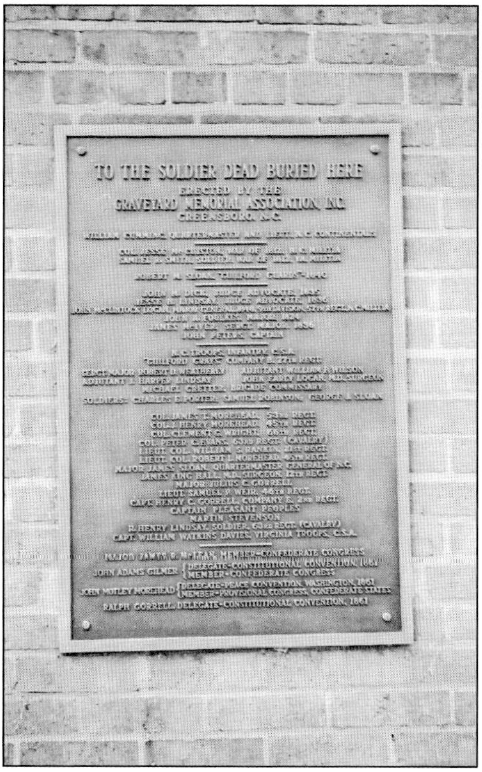

After the war, groups such as the Eclectic Club, the Ladies Memorial Association, and the Graveyard Memorial Association formed. These groups worked to provide a final resting place for the Confederate dead. The Graveyard Memorial Association erected a plaque honoring all military men buried in First Presbyterian Cemetery. The cemetery contains the graves of soldiers from four wars and the second largest group of Confederate burials in Greensboro. (CAM.)

The Ladies Memorial Association's labors resulted in a granite monument erected in Green Hill Cemetery to mark the graves of over 300 unknown soldiers. The soldiers' remains were removed from temporary burial sites in Guilford County. Supposedly there was a mass grave across from the Old Methodist Church Cemetery (no longer existing) in Greensboro. To this day, the soldiers remain known only to God. (CAM.)

Sallie Lindsay, reputed to be the most beautiful belle in antebellum Greensboro, married Col. John Alexander Gilmer of the 27th North Carolina, a former Guilford Gray, in 1864. Townspeople often spoke of the wedding of these two childhood sweethearts. The beautiful Sallie assisting her beloved John, who walked with the aid of crutches from wounds he received in battle, touched the hearts of all. (GHMAI.)

Col. John Gilmer, upon leaving his position in the army due to war injuries, retired to the invalid corps. Gilmer took charge of the Confederate prison camp in Salisbury, North Carolina. Due to health problems, he resigned as commander at the prison. The prison housed prisoners of war, Federal deserters, and Confederate soldiers under court-martial. Rumors spread of inhumanity

in the prison. In late 1864, conditions became deplorable when the prison population swelled to 10,321. Meeting the needs of so many men was impossible. Rioting broke out. Murder was committed. Men starved. Shown is a lithograph of Salisbury Prison showing Union prisoners playing baseball. (UNC.)

In 1899, the former women's groups of Greensboro merged in a common effort to pay tribute and respect to all Confederate soldiers and formed the local chapter of the United Daughters of the Confederacy. Sallie Gilmer was a charter officer of the organization. Shown is the obelisk marking the grave of John and Sallie Gilmer in Green Hill Cemetery. (CAM.)

The women of Greensboro struggled through four years of war. After the war, they continued their benevolent work. At the home of Caroline Sparrow Dalton, the women met to form a local chapter of the United Daughters of the Confederacy in Greensboro. Their chapter formed in March 1899. The women went to work as if going to battle to honor their Confederate heritage. (CAM.)

Six

Conquered Banner

A postcard scene depicts Richmond, Virginia, burning and in chaos. In April 1865, war refugees, both free and slave, fled the city in terror of losing their lives. President Davis and his cabinet fled the city by train. Rioters and evacuating Confederate soldiers damaged the city. Yankee soldiers frantically attempted to extinguish fires in hopes of saving the city. Several of the refugees ended up in Greensboro. (CAM.)

This postcard image of Libby Prison in Richmond, Virginia, depicts a building used during the war by the Confederacy as a hospital for Union prisoners. After the fall of Richmond in 1865, the United States released the prisoners but continued to use the facility as a prison for the soldiers of the surrendered Confederate army. (CAM.)

Gen. Robert E. Lee forewarned the authorities to evacuate the cities of Petersburg and Richmond, Virginia. Lee could no longer hold his position against Gen. Ulysses S. Grant. Pres. Jefferson Davis, his cabinet, and a host of refugees left Richmond by train for Danville, Virginia. Shown is a John Reekie photograph of Federal troops entering Petersburg in April 1865. (LOC.)

This 1906 postcard shows the former home of Pres. Jefferson Davis of the Confederate States of America. The house survived the war and currently houses the Museum of the Confederacy. On April 4, 1865, President Lincoln entered the home of his adversary, President Davis. (CAM.)

This Currier and Ives lithograph of the surrender at Appomattox Courthouse depicts Gen. Robert Edward Lee and Gen. Ulysses Simpson Grant sitting at a table while Lee signs the surrender documents. The men met, exchanged greetings, and talked of their life before the war. The victor and the defeated treated each other and their respective armies with respect. (LOC.)

Shown is a drawing by Alfred R. Waud of General Lee leaving the McLean House on April 9, 1865. Rations were ordered for the starving Confederate soldiers. Rumors spread in Greensboro that General Lee surrendered. Disbelief, fear, and heartache touched the citizens and soldiers in town. (LOC.)

The idea of Gen. William Tecumseh Sherman marching through North Carolina and Gen. George Stoneman invading the western portion of the state struck fear of invasion in the hearts of the citizens of Greensboro. Troops were sent to Greensboro to protect the community. Stoneman (shown) focused on destroying railroads, buildings, and supplies. (LOC.)

On April 14, 1865, John Wilkes Booth fatally shot Pres. Abraham Lincoln. Lincoln died on April 15. This event was sad news for both the North and the South. The Confederate government was under suspicion as being the driving force behind the assassination. Shown is a scene depicting the assassination of Lincoln. (LOC.)

Shown is a monument erected by Col. John Sloan Camp 1290, Sons of Confederate Veterans. It states, "Near this spot on April 13, 1865, Pres. Jefferson Davis, members of the Confederate Cabinet and Gens. Joseph E. Johnston and P. G. T. Beauregard met to discuss the Confederate military situation as a result of Gen. Robert E. Lee's surrender at Appomattox." (CAM.)

Shown is a North Carolina historical marker on Elm Street in Greensboro indicating where members of the Confederate cabinet stayed in a railroad car. Townspeople brought the men food and coffee. The townspeople offered shelter to many of the Confederate refugees besieging Greensboro. Several refugees refused shelter, fearing the invading Federal army would harm the houses and residents. (CAM.)

Shown is a postcard image of the capital of North Carolina in Raleigh. City and state officials evacuated the city in fear of the invading army. State leaders made haste to Greensboro. Legal documents were destroyed and in some cases stolen as war souvenirs. (CAM.)

Col. Zebulon Vance served in the 26th North Carolina before serving as governor and, as a result, understood the needs of the soldier in the field. He worked tirelessly, gathering clothing, food, medicine, and war supplies for the suffering soldiers in the field and the families they left behind at home. Shown from left to right are Col. John Randolph Lane, Col. Harry King Burgwyn Jr., and Col. Zebulon Baird Vance. (CLARK.)

Governor Vance (shown) fled Raleigh ahead of General Sherman's army and arrived in Greensboro on April 16, 1865. Greensboro served as the temporary capital while Vance performed his last duties as governor of North Carolina. (UNC.)

At the office of Scott and Scott, a law firm that was run by William Lafayette Scott and his brother, Levi Michael Scott (shown), Governor Vance prepared his last statements to the people of North Carolina. On April 28, 1865, in Greensboro, Vance issued his proclamation to the people of North Carolina, urging the residents to behave in a civil, peaceful manner and to remain at home. (NCMA.)

Angry citizens wanted food and supplies that were stockpiled in state and Confederate warehouses in Greensboro and insisted on receiving their share. The community erupted in rioting, gunfire, and violence. The women, their children starving, physically fought Confederate soldiers until threatened with death. Maj. James Sloan, state quartermaster in Greensboro, pleaded with Governor Vance to relieve him from his duty. Shown is Sloan's gravestone. (KEITH.)

Greensboro served as the capital of the Confederate States of America for five days. Confederate president Davis arrived in Greensboro on April 11, 1865, and addressed the citizens that greeted him. Townspeople brought him food and coffee. Davis fled Greensboro, heading south when he realized continuing the war was useless. General Stoneman destroyed the railroads leading from Greensboro; Davis and his entourage fled by horseback and carriages. (LOC.)

Shown is a Currier and Ives lithograph of Gen. Joseph E. Johnston surrendering to Gen. William Tecumseh Sherman on April 26, 1865. (LOC.)

The town experienced Johnston's Army of Tennessee encamped in and around Greensboro. Many of General Johnston's troops, injured at Bentonville, arrived in Greensboro ahead of him. Many of the men, knowing they were defeated, left for home. General Johnston bid farewell to the remnants of his army in Greensboro. Shown is Gen. Joseph E. Johnston. (LOC.)

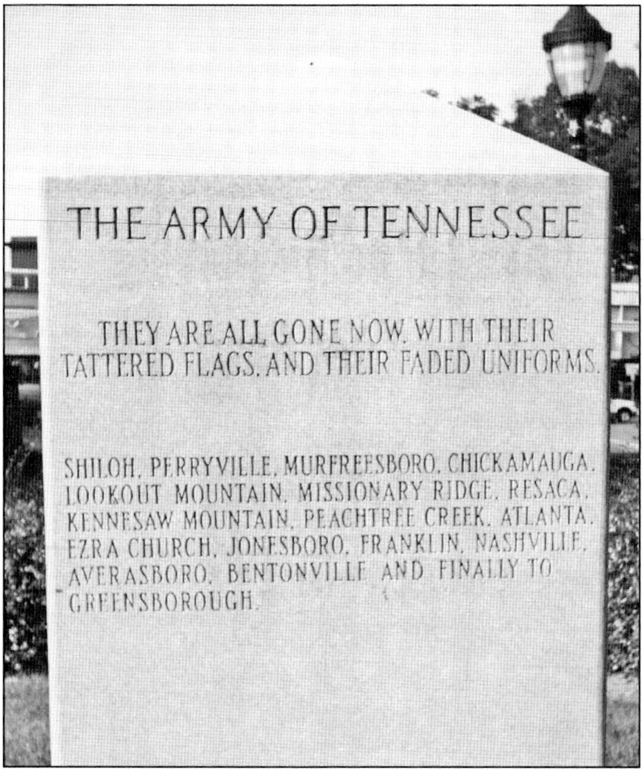

The Army of Tennessee participated in campaigns at Shiloh, Perryville, Murfreesboro, Chickamauga, Lookout Mountain, Missionary Ridge, Resaca, Kennesaw Mountain, Peachtree Creek, Atlanta, Ezra Church, Jonesboro, Franklin, Nashville, Averasboro, Bentonville, and Greensboro. Note the spelling of Greensboro as Greensborough. This monument was erected by Col. John Sloan Camp 1290, Sons of Confederate Veterans Greensboro. (CAM.)

James W. Albright recorded his experiences in his war diary. He spoke of stirring a barrel of drinking water until the bugs fell to the bottom of the barrel, at which point potable water could be obtained. Albright authored *Greensboro 1808–1904: Facts, Figures, Traditions and Reminiscences*. He collaborated with Richard Sterling and James D. Campbell to print a series of Confederate schoolbooks titled *Our Own School Books*. (CALD.)

Albright served in the 12th Virginia Battalion of Light Artillery. Before he enlisted, he printed "wallpaper scrip," so called because the notes were printed on wallpaper. Shown is a Greensboro Mutual Life Insurance and Trust Company note dated September 1, 1862, payable to Robert Paine Dick. Notice on the lower right of the note the imprint of Sterling, Campbell, and Albright, Printers. (CAM.)

Albright would easily recognize this Virginia treasury note stating it will pay the bearer $1 on demand at the treasury. As he was leaving Virginia, the Confederate Treasury ($13 million) was also fleeing the invading army. Albright and his brother were given the job of printing paroles for General Johnston's army. Albright was paid $125 dollar in U.S. currency. He wrote in his book that he felt rich. (CAM.)

Albright, looking back on his life, wrote in his book, *Greensboro 1808–1904*, "That heart, methinks were of strange mould, which kept no cherished print of earlier, happier times, when life was fresh, and love and innocence made holiday; or that owned no transient sadness when a dream, a glimpse of fancy touched past joys." Shown is the monument of James W. and Mattie Purvis Albright in Green Hill Cemetery. (CAM.)

PAROLING REBEL PRISONERS AT GREENSBOROUGH, NORTH CAROLINA.

This picture is titled *Paroling Rebel Prisoners at Greensborough, North Carolina.* Confederate soldiers entering the town looking for information, food, and paroles besieged Greensboro. Camp Stokes, located near Battleground Avenue, was a Confederate camp of instruction during the last two years of the war. It served a dual purpose as a prison for deserters and Yankee prisoners. Those incarcerated, totaling over 200 men, headed for Greensboro. Marauders, criminals, and Yankee and Rebel soldiers set up camp in Greensboro streets, cemeteries, yards, and fields. For a while, terror ruled the land; no one felt totally secure. It was necessary to tend livestock and gardens under armed guard. Women did not dare to leave the shelter of their homes. At night, war tunes touched the ears and hearts of everyone, bringing relief from the sounds heard during the day of marching troops, horses' hooves, wagons, shouted orders, and, at times, the noise of sheer mayhem; hundreds of campfires kept Greensboro lit at night. Shattered dreams and shattered lives touched every person in town. (LOC.)

The Morehead home, Blandwood, sheltered sick and wounded soldiers and high-ranking Confederate officials, and was the scene of meetings for local leaders and national leaders during the collapse of the Confederate government. The Morehead family greeted friend and foe alike with courtesy. The Morehead sons served in the Confederate army, and sons-in-law died in the service of the Confederacy. For some time, Blandwood housed the Keeley Institute; currently, it is a museum. (CAM.)

Letitia Harper Morehead Walker (shown) served as the host of Blandwood during the war. She witnessed Gen. Joseph E. Johnston bid farewell to his beloved soldiers of the Army of Tennessee after they received their paroles and greeted Confederate leaders, several of whom stayed at Blandwood. She and Julianna Gilmer were forced to witness the victorious Federal army parade through town at the request of Union general Jacob D. Cox. (CALD.)

Walker, in a program for the Greensboro Chapter of the United Daughters of the Confederacy, exclaimed, "But one fine morning, amid the sound of bugles and trumpets and bands of music, the Federals entered Greensboro, fully thirty thousand strong, to occupy the town for some time." Shown is her beloved Blandwood. (CAM.)

Shown is a *carte de visite* published by J. O'Kane of Gen. Daniel Sickles. After the surrender of the Confederate government, the defeated South was divided into five military districts under the Reconstruction Act of 1867. General Sickles, appointed by Pres. Andrew Johnson, governed the area that included North and South Carolina until 1867. (CAM.)

After the war, Northerners, labeled as carpetbaggers, arrived in Greensboro, hoping to capitalize on the plight of the defeated Southerners. Albion Tourgee, though labeled a carpetbagger, was quite wealthy. A former Union army officer from Ohio, he served as judge. He took a personal interest in the plight of the emancipated slaves. Shown is Tourgee's book, *A Fool's Errand*, published in 1879. (CAM.)

Tourgee's fictional characters were based on individuals that resided in Greensboro. The fool was Tourgee. He mistakenly thought he could help the troubled community. He also authored a book titled *Bricks without Straw*. Because of conditions in Greensboro and the Reconstruction Act, many Confederate veterans left Greensboro and migrated west. (CAM.)

After the war, William Bingham Farrar, a veteran of Company D, 35th North Carolina, moved to Greensboro. He engaged in a business making watches, clocks, and jewelry. Slowly, Greensboro citizens and Confederate veterans restored their lives and homes to normalcy. Farrar's achievements as an inventor removed him from the battlefield to the arsenal at Fayetteville, North Carolina, where his talents could be better utilized by the Confederacy. (EB.)

John Henry Dillard (1819–1896) enlisted in Company G, 45th North Carolina, reaching the rank of captain. Due to age and physical infirmities, he was no longer able to perform the duties of a soldier but remained active in the senior reserves. After the war, he moved to Greensboro, served the state as a judge, and partnered with Robert Paine Dick to form the Dick and Dillard Law School. (CALD.)

This postcard image of South Elm Street at night decades after the war shows a growing Greensboro. The years of the Reconstruction Act were over. For many citizens, though, the nights spent pacing the streets with worry, waiting for the trains to arrive with news of their loved ones, and seeing soldiers horribly wounded could never be removed from their memory and hearts. (CAM.)

Seven

In Memoriam

Memorials in the form of monuments, paintings, and treasured family pictures tell the story of the soldiers and the Confederate States of America. History records the victor in detail but omits much of the defeated. Shown is *The Confederate Note Memorial*, a work by an unknown artist predating 1902. Written on the work are the words, "Representing nothing on God's earth now; and naught in the waters below it. As the pledge of a Nation that passed away. Keep it dear friend and show it. Show it to those that will lend an ear to the tale this trifle will tell; of Liberty born of a patriot's dream, of a storm-cradled nation that fell." (LOC.)

Lauchlin J. McLean (1847–1930) enlisted in Company B, 36th North Carolina on September 26, 1864, at the age of 17. Late in the war, human resources dwindled in the South, resulting in the enlistment of younger recruits. At the Battle of Fort Fisher, North Carolina, on January 15, 1865, McLean was wounded and captured by Federal forces. He remained in prison at Point Lookout, Maryland, until June 29, 1865. A great-grandson of McLean, Don Saunders, serves as commander of Col. John Sloan Camp 1290, Sons of Confederate Veterans, in Greensboro. Shown is a picture taken around 1928 of McLean and his wife, Sara Fisher McLean (1849–1934). (DS.)

John E. Logan of the 14th North Carolina, wrote in a letter to his sister in Greensboro that "We are all astounded at the fall of Fort Fisher. We were led to believe that the place was impregnable. Certainly ought to have been. They have been at work on it long enough. The fact is the force was too small to man it." North Carolinians complained to the Confederate government that so many of their men were in Virginia fighting that it left the coast of North Carolina not sufficiently protected. Shown is Fort Fisher, photographed by Timothy H. O'Sullivan in January 1865. (LOC.)

Pvt. Samuel Vinson (shown), a soldier of Company C, 36th North Carolina Artillery, enlisted on February 26, 1862. The enemy captured him at Fort Fisher on January 15, 1865. He was taken to Point Lookout, Maryland, and imprisoned there until May 13, 1865. Vinson's comrade in arms, Pvt. Morris Hall of Company C, 36th North Carolina Artillery, enlisted on June 8, 1862, and he too was captured and taken prisoner. (BRAME.)

Hall was taken to Elmira, New York, and incarcerated as a prisoner of war until June 12, 1865. Little did Vinson and Hall know during their fight to save Fort Fisher that generations later they would share a descendant, Jack Brame, who currently serves as lieutenant commander of Col. John Sloan Camp 1290, Sons of Confederate Veterans, in Greensboro. Shown is a picture of Hall and his son, Robert, taken shortly after the war. (BRAME.)

Shown are obsolete currency notes from the State of North Carolina Treasury. One note is dated January 1, 1863, and the other is dated January 1, 1864. Both notes depict a ship on the high seas. Blockade running was a necessity for the Confederacy and the state of North Carolina as resources dwindled. (LOPP.)

The *Advance*, a blockade-runner, succeeded in delivering the plates necessary to print Confederate schoolbooks in Greensboro on her maiden voyage. Letitia Walker spoke of wearing gloves and shoes that arrived via blockade-runner. Goods from England, swapped in exchange for cotton, were necessary to the Confederacy. Walker complained of the inflated prices paid for such luxuries as new gloves and shoes. (LOPP.)

Pvt. Peter Lopp (1823–1885) enlisted in Company C, 76th North Carolina, known as the 6th North Carolina Reserves. This company consisted of older men called upon for service in the Confederate army. Before the war, Peter was a blacksmith and a farmer tending 1,000 acres. His regiment was sent to Greensboro on March 4, 1865. At General Johnston's surrender, the men left for home. (LOPP.)

Peter's brother, Pvt. Jacob Lopp, enlisted in the Lexington Wildcats, 4th North Carolina Volunteers, later designated as Company I, 14th North Carolina. Jacob suffered an arm wound at Gettysburg on July 1, 1863. After the Battle of Gettysburg, he was held as a prisoner of war until February 18, 1865, at which time he was exchanged and sent to Camp Lee, Virginia. (LOPP.)

Jacob's brother, Pvt. Mathias Lopp, enlisted in the same company as his brother. Jane Lopp Brame, a resident of Guilford County, is the great-granddaughter of Peter. Jacob and Mathias Lopp are her great-great-uncles. Jane is a member of the United Daughters of the Confederacy and a member of the Order of Confederate Rose. It was common for families to send more than one son to the battlefields in defense of home. (LOPP.)

Sgt. Hiram Randall Berrier (1839–1910) served with the Carolina Rangers, Company B, 10th Virginia Cavalry. Berrier was wounded on June 25, 1864. The severe wound resulted in the amputation of his right leg. Berrier is described as having dark hair, gray eyes, and a fair complexion. He stood 5 feet, 6 inches tall. After the war, North Carolina offered artificial limbs to Confederate and state amputees, including Berrier. (LOPP.)

Pvt. Daniel Wilson Jones, Company F, 2nd North Carolina Cavalry (19th Regiment North Carolina Troops) was born in Stokes County in 1842. He enlisted in High Point, North Carolina, on June 18, 1861. After the war, he moved to Stokesdale in Guilford County, married Sarah Crews in 1872, and raised 13 children. William "Bill" Jones, a great-grandson of Daniel, relates, "Jones was granted a disability Soldier's Pension in 1885 due to his nagging leg injury and had his leg amputated just below the knee in 1890. He wore a wooden leg thereafter and was referred to by his neighbor as 'Peg-Leg.'" Shown is Daniel in his uniform. (JONES.)

William "Bill" Jones shares additional information: "The 2nd North Carolina Calvary participated in scouting and flanking movements during the Battle of Chancellorville, Virginia, in early May 1863, and then the largest cavalry battle of the entire war at Brandy Station, Virginia, on June 9, 1863. Jones was wounded during this battle and was sent to Chimborazo Hospital No. 3 in Richmond. On June 22, 1863, he was transferred to Salisbury for further recovery. Jones's leg wound was serious enough for him to be retired to the invalid corps on January 6, 1865." Shown is the Daniel Wilson Jones family, from left to right: (first row) Elizabeth, Robert, Zeb, and Bohnson; (second row) George, Daniel Wilson, Sara Jane, Mollie, and Nora; (third row) Virgil Oran, Daniel Arthur, Buford, Jo Mattie, and Lura. (JONES.)

Shown are Jones and his daughters Lizzie (holding the puppy) and Nora. Notice the girls' hair, with a straight part down the center of their heads. This hairstyle was popular throughout the war era and for decades afterward. Descendants of Jones are active in patriotic organizations to this day in Guilford County. (JONES.)

For some Confederate soldiers, only their monuments tell the story of their war experiences. Thomas A. Grissom, Company B, 52nd North Carolina, was born in Tennessee and was a farmer in Randolph County, North Carolina, at the onset of the War Between the States. Carved on Grissom's monument is "He served four years in the / Confederate Army. Was / shot through the lung / at Bristow, Va. from which / he never fully recovered." (CAM.)

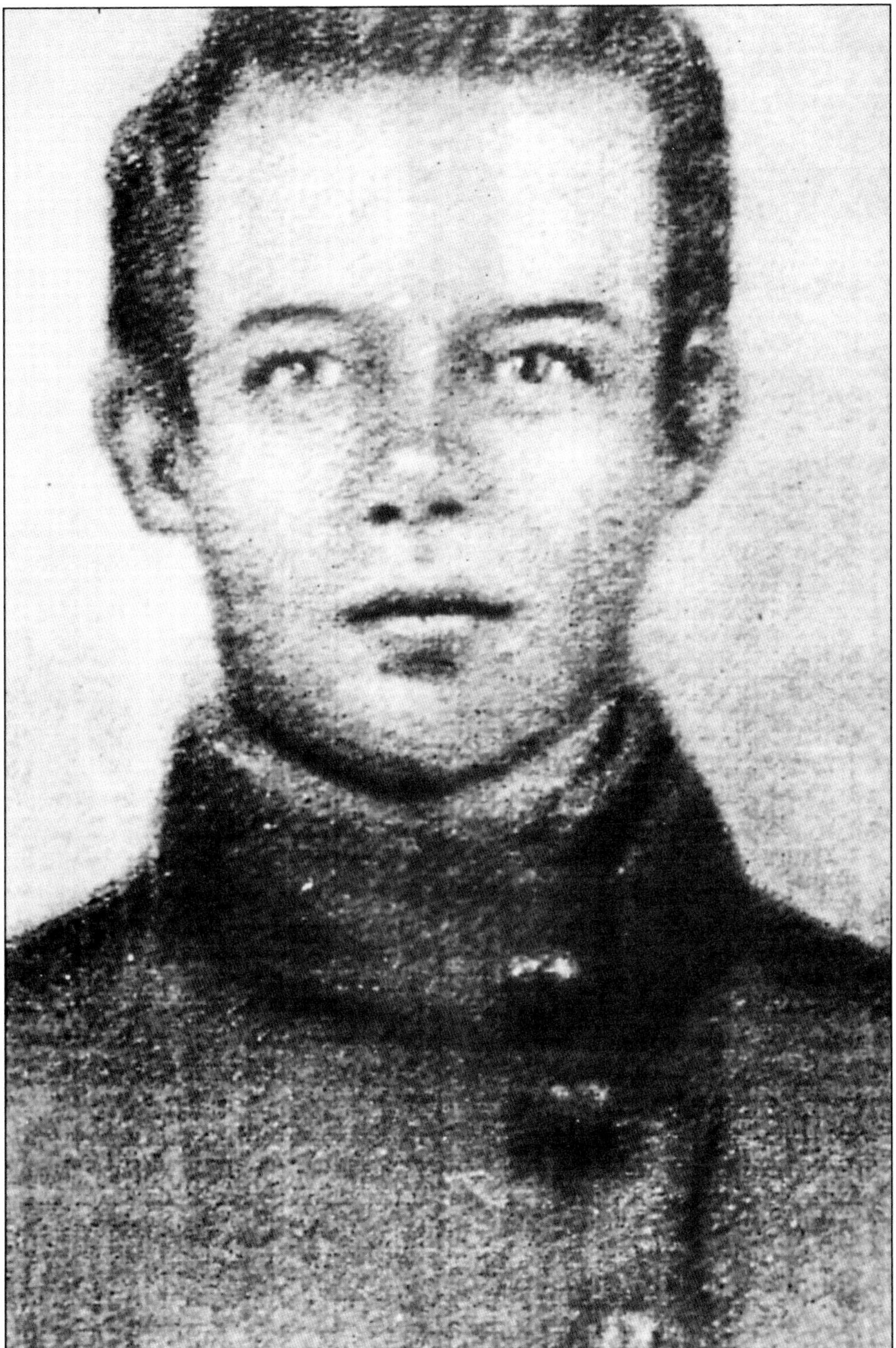

Robert Sanders Phipps (shown) enlisted in the North Carolina Militia in 1863 at the age of 17. He transferred to Freeman's Battalion and trained to be a prison guard at the Confederate prison camp in Salisbury, North Carolina. He was taken prisoner during General Stoneman's raid. After his release, he walked to Greensboro. In 1870, Phipps married Mary Anna Gilmer and fathered seven children. He married Sallie Virginia Browning in 1907 and had five children. (JS.)

Shown is the Phipps family home in McLeansville built during the war. The home place originally consisted of hundreds of acres of land. The detached kitchen burned many years ago. The home has been preserved by the family for generations. Phipps's daughter, Effie Claire Phipps Whittle, resides in Guilford County, one of the few remaining real daughters of the United Daughters of the Confederacy. (CAM.)

The Phipps family history tells of visits by officers of the Union army who asked the family for food. While hosting the officers, the family faced thieving marauders intent on stealing and destroying their property. The Union officers assisted the family in protecting their property. A granddaughter, Joanne Sharpe, is current president of Guilford Chapter 301, United Daughters of the Confederacy. (CAM.)

This photograph from an ambrotype of Pvt. Robert Patterson, Company D, 12th Tennessee Infantry was chosen to represent all Tennesseans that served the Confederate States of America. The 12th Tennessee was paroled on May 2, 1865, in Greensboro during General Johnston's surrender. General Johnston surrendered over 90,000 troops. (LOC.)

Shown is the military marker located in Tollison's Cemetery in White County, Tennessee, of Pvt. William L. Baker, Company B, 1st Tennessee Infantry. Baker was a farmer. Remnants of his company were paroled in Greensboro. Many Tennesseans in Gen. Joseph E. Johnston's Army of Tennessee in May 1865 became Greensboro's Confederate soldiers. Descendants of Baker reside in Guilford County. (CAM.)

The United Confederate Veterans officially organized in New Orleans, Louisiana, on June 10, 1889; Guilford Chapter 795 organized on October 5, 1896, at a meeting held at the Guilford County courthouse. James T. Morehead, William S. Rankin, Jesse R. Wharton, Thomas Rhodes, Thomas J. Sloan, and others united with veterans from many states to form the chapter. Confederate Memorial Day celebrations, held annually in Greensboro on May 10, were celebrated in 1896 with a trip to

Green Hill Cemetery, where the graves of Confederate dead were covered with flowers. In August 1902, the annual state reunion of the United Confederate Veterans held in Greensboro attracted over 1,200 participants. Tents set up at Davie and Washington Streets helped to accommodate the visitors. This reunion picture shows the members of Guilford Chapter 795, United Confederate Veterans, in front of the First Presbyterian Church in Greensboro. (GHMAI.)

On May 10, 1905, the annual meeting of the United Confederate Veterans was held at the Grand Opera House. Several veterans received Southern Crosses of Honor bestowed from the hand of a Daughter of the Confederacy. After the ceremony, the veterans—some on foot, others in carriages—paraded to Green Hill Cemetery to discover that children, under the direction of the United Daughters of the Confederacy, had adorned the Confederate graves with flowers. After prayers, the customary salute to the dead was performed. Shown is Green Hill Cemetery. The obelisk monument honoring Col. John A. Gilmer, a member of the 27th North Carolina, is in the left foreground. (CAM.)

In 1896, Tom Sloan, a former Guilford Gray, served as a recruiting officer for the Confederate veterans being organized in Greensboro. As many as 200 men enlisted for inclusion in the newly former United Confederate Veteran Chapter 795. Charter members, though predominately from North Carolina, included veterans from Virginia, Texas, South Carolina, Louisiana, Kentucky, and Arkansas. Shown here are North Carolina Confederate veterans parading in Washington, D.C., during a 1917 reunion. North Carolina is known as the "Tar Heel" state, and North Carolinians are referred to as "Tar Heels."

Walter D. McAdoo, one of the charter members of Camp 795, United Confederate Veterans, served in the Guilford Grays and Company A, 53rd North Carolina. McAdoo, wounded at Sharpsburg, Maryland, and at Gettysburg, Pennsylvania, and taken prisoner, was exchanged and eventually retired to the invalid corps in Greensboro. He survived the war and received his parole in Greensboro in May 1865 during General Johnston's surrender. His gravestone is shown. (CAM.)

The McAdoo Hotel was established by McAdoo. In 1881, the hotel was the scene of a reunion banquet consisting of veteran Guilford Grays and sons of Guilford Grays. The Guilford Grays formed and reformed throughout the 19th and 20th centuries to honor ancestors, teach Southern history, and to protect Greensboro and the United States. (CAM.)

After the war, remains of the dead were buried in trench graves and cemeteries throughout Guilford County. Three hundred Confederate soldiers died without any identification. Their remains were gathered and buried in a mass grave at Green Hill Cemetery. Through the efforts of the Ladies Memorial Association, a monument marks the graves of the soldiers. (CAM.)

The monument, vandalized, was elevated to help preserve it. The Ladies Memorial Association originally erected it; the Sons of Confederate Veterans and the United Daughters of the Confederacy have memorial and commemorative services at the location. Shown are images of the front and the rarely photographed back of the monument. Note the letters "CSA" carved on the soldier's cartridge box. (CAM.)

People gather at the monument on November 17, 2007, to pay their respects to the dead and dedicate an additional inscription. Carved on the monument is "Our Confederate dead / 1861–1865 / dedicated in the / memory of / 300 unknown soldiers / by the Ladies' / Memorial Asso. of / Greensboro, NC." These words were added: "which became / Daughters of the Confederacy / Guilford Chapter 301, 1899." (CAM.)

Shown is a Confederate monument in Hollywood Cemetery in Richmond, Virginia, honoring the memory of 18,000 soldiers. Monuments in honor of fallen Confederate soldiers were erected throughout the South. Many of the monuments were the result of efforts by women. (CAM.)

Shown is the Confederate president Jefferson Davis monument in Hollywood Cemetery. The monument in the foreground is in honor of Davis's daughter, Winnie, erected by the United Daughters of the Confederacy. (CAM.)

This Confederate monument in Raleigh honors all Confederate soldiers from North Carolina that served in the Confederate States of America. (CAM.)

Capt. John A. Sloan, a Guilford Gray, wrote, "On each return of spring, come and bring flowers, nature's choicest, and scatter them on their graves. So long as tears fall, come and shed them there, and show to the world that we, of all men, are not ashamed of their memory or afraid to vindicate their motives. And as we stand upon this hallow ground, let us bury all animosities engendered by the war. In the grave there can be no rancorous hates; between the sleepers there is perpetual truce. Shall the living have less? Savages, only, perpetuate immortal hates. Then permit no 'barbarian memory of wrong' to lodge in our breast while we keep vigils over these graves of our illustrious dead." (CAM.)

Shown is First Presbyterian Cemetery in Greensboro. The tall obelisk in the background of this picture marks the final resting place of members of John A. Sloan's family. Three members of the Confederate Congress are buried in the cemetery: John Motley Morehead, John Adams Gilmer, and James Robert McLean. Maj. James Sloan, state Confederate quartermaster; Ralph Gorrell, depositary; and Jesse H. Lindsay handled matters affecting the Confederate Treasury locally. (CAM.)

Confederate veteran graves exist in cemeteries throughout Guilford County. Green Hill Cemetery has more Confederate graves than all the others combined in Greensboro. First Presbyterian Cemetery has a large number of Confederate graves, many of which are no longer marked with monuments. In the background of the picture is the monument of Dr. John Early Logan, 14th North Carolina. (CAM.)

Decades after the war, this patriotic postcard, mailed in 1907, pays honor to all soldiers that participated in the War Between the States. "From the silence of sorrowful hours, the desolate mourners go, lovingly laden with flowers, alike for the friend and the foe: under the sod and the dew, waiting the judgment day, under the roses the blue, under the lilies the gray." I pledge allegiance to the flag of the United States of America, and to the republic for which it stands one nation, under God, indivisible with liberty and justice for all. May freedom always be the binding thread that unites the United States of America! (CAM.)

BIBLIOGRAPHY

Albright, James W., comp. *Greensboro 1808–1904: Facts, Figures, Traditions, and Reminiscences.* 1904. Reprint, Salem, MA: Higginson Book Company, 1904.

Arnett, Ethel Stephens. *Confederate Guns Were Stacked Greensboro, North Carolina.* Greensboro, NC: Piedmont Press, 1965.

Bridges, Earley Winfred. *Greensboro Lodge No. 76 A. F. & A. M.* Staunton, VA: McClure Printing Company, 1951.

Caldwell, Bettie D., comp. *Founders and Builders of Greensboro 1808–1908: Fifty Sketches.* Greensboro, NC: Jos. J. Stone and Company, 1925.

Clark, Walter, ed. *Histories of the Several Regiments and Battalions from North Carolina in the Great War, 1861–1865, Written by Members of the Respective Commands.* 5 vol. Wilmington, NC: Broadfoot Publishing Company, 1996.

Greensboro Daily News.

Greensboro *Patriot.*

Greensboro Public Library.

Konkle, Burton A. *John Motley Morehead and the Development of North Carolina 1796–1866.* Philadelphia: William J. Campbell, 1922.

Long, Mary Alves. *High Time to Tell It.* Durham, NC: Duke, 1950.

Manarin, Louis H., comp. *North Carolina Troops, 1861–1865; a Roster.* Vol. 1–15, Raleigh, NC: State Department of Archives and History, 1966.

Moore, Carol. *Greensboro's First Presbyterian Church Cemetery.* Charleston, SC: Arcadia Publishing, 2006.

National Archives and Records Administration.

Simpson, John Wells. *History of the First Presbyterian Church of Greensboro, N.C. 1824–1945.* Greensboro, N.C.: privately printed, 1945.

Sloan, John A. *Reminiscences of the Guilford Grays: Company B, 27th NC Regiment.* Washington, D.C.: R. O. Polkinhorn, printer, 1883.

Stockard, Sallie W. *The History of Guilford County, North Carolina.* Knoxville, TN: Gaut-Ogden Company, 1902.

Weatherly, Andrew Earl. *The First Hundred Years of Historic Guilford, 1771–1871.* Greensboro, NC: Greensboro Print Company, 1972.

ACROSS AMERICA, PEOPLE ARE DISCOVERING SOMETHING WONDERFUL. *THEIR HERITAGE.*